KT-151-851
High Life Highland

APR 2016

BE YOUR OWN
ASTROLOGER

UNLOCK THE SECRETS OF
THE SIGNS AND PLANETS

HIGH LIFE
HIGHLAND

3800 18 0078049 0	
Askews & Holts	16-Jan-2019
133.5	£7.99

WITHDRAWN

JOANNA WATTERS

CICO BOOKS
LONDON NEW YORK

*This book is dedicated to Paul Hitchings and Ronnie Lloyd,
whose combined worldly and spiritual wisdom has seen me
through every challenge of my life and taught me so much
over the last 30 years. Without you my work would lack the
depth that I hope I have achieved, and I dedicate this book
to both of you with all my love and gratitude.*

This edition published in 2018 by CICO Books
an imprint of Ryland Peters & Small Ltd
20–21 Jockey's Fields   341 E 116th St
London WC1R 4BW   New York, NY 10029

www.rylandpeters.com

First published in 2015

10 9 8 7 6 5 4 3 2 1

Text © Joanna Watters 2015, 2018
Design and illustration © CICO Books 2015, 2018

The author's moral rights have been asserted. All rights
reserved. No part of this publication may be reproduced,
stored in a retrieval system, or transmitted in any form or
by any means, electronic, mechanical, photocopying, or
otherwise, without the prior permission of the publisher.

A CIP catalog record for this book is available from the
Library of Congress and the British Library.

ISBN: 978-1-78249-655-7

Printed in China

Editor: Jennifer Jahn
Design concept: Emily Breen
Illustrator: Sarah Perkins

Commissioning editor: Kristine Pidkameny
Senior editor: Carmel Edmonds
Junior designer: Eliana Holder
Art director: Sally Powell
Production controller: Mai-Ling Collyer
Publishing manager: Penny Craig
Publisher: Cindy Richards

CONTENTS

INTRODUCTION

The road to astrology is paved with misconceptions, which are largely down to the fact that the gap between Sun-sign astrology and horoscopy is immense. While the former is kept alive and kicking in media horoscopes, often referred to as "Your Stars," the latter is the study of the individual horoscope, also known as the birth chart or the nativity. Your stars in a newspaper or magazine or on a website are not in fact your "horoscope," but an astrologer's "take" on the current planetary activity. Even when written professionally, such columns can only generalize; they still wear the fortune

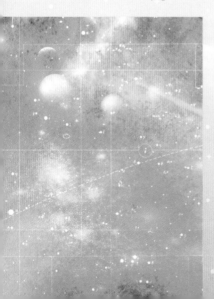

teller's hat and are inevitably branded in the public eye as entertainment. On the other hand, the study of your own birth chart means unlocking a treasure trove of self-awareness, guidance, insights, and deep

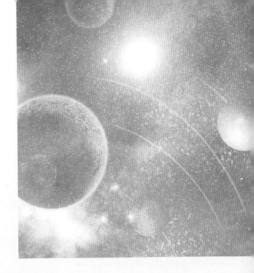

understanding of how you came into this world, your psychological makeup, your purpose in this life, and the nature of the relationships and experiences that you will encounter along your way.

We all have our own individual horoscope, a chart that is unique to us and that is calculated from our personal data of date, place, and time of birth. Nobody else's chart can be identical to our own unless that other person is born on exactly the same day, in the same place, and at the same time. While we all know our Sun sign, none of us can know our Moon sign, Mercury sign, Venus sign, and so on without consulting an Ephemerides, a book containing the planetary timetables that tell us which planet is in which sign on any given day. Furthermore, none of us can

know our Ascendant—
or Rising Sign—without
knowing our time of birth
and calculating the whole
horoscope.

In the past, the craft of
calculating the horoscope
required the skills of a trained
astrologer, but modern-day
technology has changed
this forever. Now the
mathematical exercise of
erecting a horoscope based
on the exact data of an
individual's date, place, and time of birth can be done online
in a matter of minutes. You can find out more about
calculating your horoscope in Chapter Four (see page 152),
along with recommended websites for doing this.

Having armed yourself with your horoscope, however, is
where the value of astrological software ends. Putting it
another way, this is where the worlds of astronomy and
astrology divide. At an objective and mathematical level, the

horoscope is generated from specific data and is firmly rooted in time and space, but at a subjective and symbolic level, the horoscope holds destiny's DNA that awaits to be unraveled and decoded.

The main focus of this book, then, is to lead the reader along the road that starts with objective information and ends with particular meaning. No software in the world can take you on that journey, as the act of interpretation—the reading of your unique astrological DNA—can be achieved only when the horoscope is aligned with context. In other words, the craft of horoscopy shows us how to marry astrological symbolism with the uniqueness of an individual's life story. Every craft needs learning and honing, and in these pages lie the tools of the astrologer's trade.

Horoscopy therefore is not clairvoyance.

But it is magic.

CHAPTER 1
SUN SIGNS

All astrology starts with Sun signs. At some point in your childhood you will have learned your Sun sign and, as with your own name, you almost certainly do not remember the exact moment at which you learned it. It is simply part of your identity and, somehow, even without any conscious studying, some of the key characteristics associated with your sign probably also came to be part of this unconsciously acquired knowledge.

A STARTING POINT

The horoscope shows us that we are all, in fact, a mixture of signs, but the Sun sign is nevertheless always a central consideration. The Sun symbolizes our essential self, the core of our personality and purpose around which everything else revolves. This may appear to suggest that we all can be easily pigeonholed, but, as you read on, you will discover that the study of any individual horoscope reveals that this is actually very far from the truth. The extent to which you find that you are "typical" of your Sun sign is less a definitive test of astrology's accuracy than an issue that is determined by the condition of the Sun in your natal horoscope. In other words, the key characteristics of your sign will be modified to a greater or lesser extent depending on the position of the Sun in your horoscope and how it is connected to the other planets. This is further explored in Chapter Three (The Houses, see page 136).

The biggest stumbling block of astrological literature is to state any kind of interpretation as if it were a given. This results only in the creation of myths rather than meaningful information, such as "all earth signs are practical," or "all fire signs are spontaneous." Such statements are obviously over-simplified and easy to dismantle. We all know earth-sign individuals who do not know one end of a screwdriver from another or fire-sign people who are not risk takers.

The following illustrations of the twelve signs of the zodiac are therefore designed to encapsulate their core meaning. The characteristics of the signs with regard to physical appearance, nature, aptitudes, and needs are based on tradition—the astrological knowledge that has been handed down to us over thousands of years—and also on my own observations and findings through client work and research that spans nearly 30 years.

 Most importantly, a sound grasp of the symbolism of the twelve signs is the bedrock of astrological interpretation and goes way beyond an understanding of just the Sun sign. However, learning to think symbolically starts with the Sun signs and is crucial to the understanding of the craft of horoscopy. One of my favorite phrases when I am teaching is that "the chart is the individual, the individual is the chart." In other words, you are your chart. Astrology is not causal. No planet makes you into the kind of person that you are or dictates that you behave in a certain way. More accurately, the horoscope is a celestial mirror. Look into it, and it will reflect back to you your life, your purpose, your relationships, your vocation, your health, and so on.

THE
ELEMENTS AND MODES

Think of the horoscope as an onion. Sun signs are the outer wrapper, covering many other layers that lead us into the heart of any individual chart. The natural symmetry of the horoscope, and the realization that everything in astrology is connected, starts to unfold as soon as we look at the Sun signs in terms of the distribution of elements and modes.

The assignment of an element and mode further singularizes the signs, illustrating and refining their essential temperament and the ways in which it is expressed.

ELEMENTS

The four astrological elements are fire, earth, air, and water. Every fourth sign shares the same element, so there are three signs for each. These are known as the triplicities.

If you join up any three signs of the same triplicity, you will create an equilateral triangle. This is the first stepping stone towards understanding the relationship between signs. For now, note that signs sharing the same element are in trine with one another; that is, they are compatible or harmonious —think "being in your element."

FIRE

The Fire triplicity:
Aries, Leo, Sagittarius
Characteristics:
warmth, passion,
vision, intuition

EARTH

The Earth triplicity:
Taurus, Virgo,
Capricorn
Characteristics:
sensuality, practicality,
fertility, materialism

AIR

The Air triplicity:
Gemini, Libra,
Aquarius
Characteristics:
thought, intellect,
ideas, interaction

WATER

The Water triplicity:
Cancer, Scorpio,
Pisces
Characteristics:
feelings, sensitivity,
empathy, instinct

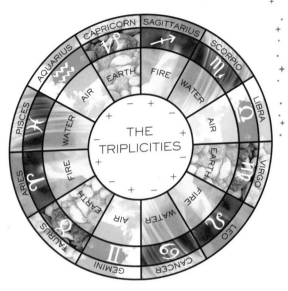

MASCULINE AND FEMININE SIGNS

Every fire and air sign is masculine (+) and every
earth and water sign is feminine (−). These are
also referred to as positive or negative, but not in
any "good or bad" sense—think yin-yang energy,
which describes how opposite forces are not only
complementary but also interdependent. In the same
way, the Sun and Moon are another example, as it
would be impossible to have night without day.

LINKS TO THE PSYCHE

Swiss psychiatrist and psychotherapist Carl Jung had a lifelong interest in astrology. The four cognitive functions of the psyche, which he conceived originally, correlate directly with the four elements. The links between the psyche and the elements can be delineated as follows:

FIRE: INTUITION
Intuitives find meaning through what may be termed non-rational information, such as hunches or visions. They can make leaps of imagination or connect their insights in a way that leads to "I just know" answers.

EARTH: SENSATION
Sensates find meaning through rational information as gathered through the five senses of sight, taste, touch, sound, and smell. Their world is one of concrete reality in which a sixth sense is either absent or disregarded.

AIR: THINKING
Thinkers find meaning through rational information, such as facts and figures. They operate by what makes sense; they look for logical connections and are disorientated by people or matters that they cannot understand.

WATER: FEELING
Feelers find meaning through non-rational information and operate purely on the basis of how someone or something makes them feel. They react emotionally and base their judgments on pleasant or unpleasant impressions.

MODES

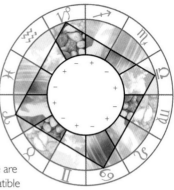

The three astrological modes are cardinal, fixed, and mutable. Every third sign shares the same mode, so there are four signs for each. These are known as the quadruplicities.

If you join up any four signs of the same quadruplicity, you will create a square. For now, note that signs sharing the same mode are in "square" to one another and are incompatible or inharmonious.

CARDINAL

Cardinal quadruplicity: Aries, Cancer, Libra, Capricorn
This mode represents the element in its most concentrated or active form. It is associated with push, energy, and initiation.

FIXED

Fixed quadruplicity: Taurus, Leo, Scorpio, Aquarius
As the name suggests, this mode represents the element in its least changeable form. It is associated with stability or stubbornness.

MUTABLE

Mutable quadruplicity: Gemini, Virgo, Sagittarius, Pisces
Sometimes called "common," this mode represents the element at its most fluid. It is associated with flexibility, movement, and the dissemination of energy.

♈ ARIES
(MARCH 21–APRIL 20)

SYMBOL: **The Ram**

RULING PLANET: **Mars**

ELEMENT AND MODE: **Cardinal Fire (masculine)**

SPOT THE ARIES

Aries rules the head and the face and you can often recognize this sign by the sharp profile, high cheekbones, aquiline nose, and firm jaw. Look for a scar on the face, too. When you meet an Aries they tend to look you straight in the eye and ask direct and highly interested questions. They are the masters of giving undivided attention, even if they do quickly move on to the next person or the next topic of interest. Mars' color red is also a big clue. It is quite astonishing how many Aries people are red-haired. You will also find that most Aries women have dyed their hair red at some point in their life, even if it does not suit them. What does suit them is a hat. Baseball caps are a favorite, but they can carry off any kind of headwear, from beach sombreros to an Ascot creation.

THE ARIES NATURE

As the first sign of the zodiac, Aries people are initiators. They thrive on action and immediacy and are energetic, impatient, and direct. They are the first to volunteer to do something, and they do it straight away. They have a knack of getting straight to the point and finding a positive answer. This is the sign of the ego, so they are also competitive and tend to regard second place as one for losers. This can be coupled with irreverence—or even total disregard for the "rules"—as they know that giving too much weight to what others might think will hold them back. Here, then, is the archetype of the pioneer and the trailblazer. Just because something has never been done before does not mean that it cannot be done now. In

fact, the challenge of "finding a way" and tucking a "first" under their belt is irresistible for this can-do sign.

LOVE AND RELATIONSHIPS

It is not unusual to find that the Aries' courage often wavers when venturing into emotional territory. The fear of rejection is the fear of failure—and to feel ridiculous is an Aries nightmare. They are also speed freaks, and it is practically a knee-jerk reaction to up the tempo and race to a conclusion. In this respect, it is difficult for them to endure the courtship stage and, once partnered, they then have to learn

IN A NUTSHELL

immediate
incisive
direct
innovative
inspirational
effective

KEY PHRASE

"I am"

that the "let's compromise and do it my way" approach does not work. Their opposite sign of Libra—the sign of balance, partnership, and arbitration—embodies the natural skills and arts of relating that Aries has to acquire.

Generally, for an Aries to be happy in love, there must never be any risk of playing second fiddle. Love triangles are a no-no, as are long-distance relationships. The need to feel special and prized is an essential ingredient in the Aries life and, in their love life, it is indispensable.

VOCATION

Fiercely independent, those born under this Mars sign are not ideally suited for teamwork (unless they happen to be team leader). They are generally self-starters and are capable of phenomenal single-mindedness. They are "project people" and therefore unlikely to stay in the same job for years on end.

Whatever their chosen profession, the Aries goal is not just to achieve but to excel, and at some point in the conversation they usually manage to tell you how good they are at their job. They are absolutely brilliant at self-advertisement; they believe in hard work and striving for what they want and have little time for moaners and complainers.

The flip side of the Aries coin is the "self"-ish streak and a capacity for diva behavior. But when they are fired up with a worthwhile cause, it is a completely different story. Suddenly the tables are turned and they are selfless as an inspirer or role model. As natural defenders, they will move mountains to help someone in genuine need. Many Aries people are in caring professions that require fight as opposed to pity, such as social work or human rights. They are natural born crusaders and delight in making a difference.

HEALTH

A typical Aries does not need any instructions when it comes to living it up, but all fire signs have to be careful of "burnout." It is too easy for this sign to burn the candle at both ends, and they have to learn to slow down

TEXTBOOK ARIES

Journalist and broadcaster **Piers Morgan** (b. March 30, 1965), whose career is peppered with controversy and clashes of ego. From early 2011 until March 2014, he presented *Piers Morgan Live* on CNN.

Anne Sullivan (April 14, 1866–October 20, 1936), who—as savior, teacher, and lifelong companion—devoted her life to deaf and blind Helen Keller, as portrayed in the 1982 movie *The Miracle Worker*.

Reba McEntire (b. March 28, 1955) aka "Big Red," the first singer to win the Country Music Association's Female Vocalist of the Year Award four consecutive times, and the only female to achieve solo number ones across four decades in the US.

occasionally to recharge their batteries. Early warning signs of depletion are headaches, migraines, or sinusitis. Aries people are prone to all Mars' heat-related conditions, such as burns, fevers, rashes and inflammation, bites or stings, injuries incurred through haste, such as cuts or grazes, sports injuries, or strains to the body incurred when not recognizing their physical limitations.

♉ TAURUS
(APRIL 21–MAY 21)

SYMBOL: **The Bull**
RULING PLANET: **Venus**
ELEMENT AND MODE: **Fixed Earth (feminine)**

SPOT THE TAURUS

Taurus rules the neck. You will occasionally come across the long swan variety, but more usually Taureans are distinguishable by the short, muscular "bull" neck atop broad shoulders. Their faces bear an uncanny resemblance to cows, in the nicest possible sense. Look for the bovine square face, the gentle eyes, and that thoughtful look that they adopt as they chew the cud. The men tend to have strong, solid bodies and are barrel-chested with pronounced square chins. The women can be either stocky or tall but are usually exceptionally feminine—look for the ribbons and bows. When untroubled, both sexes ooze serenity, softness, and sensuality.

THE TAURUS NATURE

The typical Taurus nature is steady and unhurried. Patient, kind, and good-natured, their approach is slow and deliberate, and they tend to be risk-averse. They are usually at their best when able to do things in their own way and in their own time, or if arrangements are made with plenty of warning. On a bad day, they are slow to the point of inertia, lazy, or just plain obstinate. If you try to rush them, they will dig their heels in even deeper. When they are goaded, which usually takes extreme provocation, you will see the steely glint in the eye or witness the raging bull in full explosion. Leave them well alone for up to three days.

When dealing with a crisis, they stay serene under pressure. They have huge reserves of common sense and will click into sensible mode and deal with matters in a hands-on way. Tolerance and droll humor are their saving graces, and they can be hilariously funny.

LOVE AND RELATIONSHIPS

With their own brand of earthy charm and humor, Taureans can be incredibly sociable and entertaining. This, however, sometimes gives the wrong impression in the dating game. Their dislike of being pushed or pressured definitely extends to their love life. Their sensual appetite means that they are perfectly capable of having flings like everyone else, but they are probably the least likely sign to enter into a committed

IN A NUTSHELL

stoical
reliable
sensuous
appetitive
tolerant
risk-averse

KEY PHRASE

"I possess"

relationship in haste. Their top must-have is safety, and the slightest hint of insincerity or behavior that makes them feel uncomfortable is enough to prompt a huge step back.

Once in love, Taureans make loyal partners. They tend to live and let live rather than find fault, they have a long fuse, and they value the relaxation, loving sex, and companionship of genuine attachment. The flip side of the coin is that they can endure discontent for a long time and, just as they are slow to commit, they are also slow to leave. This earth sign finds it hard to climb out of ruts, often preferring familiarity and financial security to the lure of new adventures.

VOCATION

Persistent and pragmatic, Taureans can turn their hands to pretty much anything. Being connoisseurs of comfort, security, and retail therapy, they dislike constantly having to make ends meet. They would rather slog away at something menial than be broke, but there is always the danger of creating and staying in that legendary Taurus rut as a result.

Together, the sign of Taurus and ruling planet Venus govern money, produce, women, and beauty. Job satisfaction is important for this sign and is often discovered through a connection with nature. Taureans do not mind getting their hands dirty, and here we find them in the farming and food industries, as well as pottery and floristry. Many Taureans are talented artists with a sensual feel for fabrics and designs. The financial sector also provides traditional Taurus roles.

With the Taurus rulership of the throat, many Taureans are drawn to the music industry. In particular, this sign tends to produce distinctive singers.

HEALTH

Those born under the sign of the Bull tend to be hardy creatures, usually enjoying robust health and escaping minor ailments to which others are prone. Their stamina levels tend to be higher than average, or they are simply good at pacing themselves. What may come across as laziness is

TEXTBOOK TAUREANS

Singer **Kelly Clarkson** (b. April 24, 1982), who, with her powerful, growly voice, sang her way to victory in the first *American Idol*, and whose continually fluctuating weight became a subject of obsessive media scrutiny.

Jay Leno (b. April 28, 1950), comedian and television host whose autobiography is called *Leading with my Chin*. He has donated thousands to the charity Feminist Majority, to help the plight of women in Afghanistan.

Donatella Versace (b. May 2, 1955), vice president and chief designer at Versace, who took the helm to continue her brother Gianni Versace's legacy and empire after his untimely death.

often a type of built-in physical regulator, allowing them to meet the physical demands on their body by expending the minimum amount of energy required.

When their immune system does let them down, this sign is susceptible to sore throats, tonsillitis, laryngitis, swollen glands, and problems related to the vocal chords or thyroid. This sign also rules the gums and the middle ear. Weight is the other issue. As the sign of the senses, they are often comfort eaters and can pile on the pounds.

♊ GEMINI

(MAY 22–JUNE 21)

SYMBOL: **The Twins**

RULING PLANET: **Mercury**

ELEMENT AND MODE: **Mutable Air (masculine)**

SPOT THE GEMINI

Gemini rules the lungs, nervous system, shoulders, arms, and hands. You can often spot this excitable sign by the way they gesticulate in order to express themselves. As the communicators of the zodiac, talking is as natural as breathing, but if you asked them to sit on their hands, most Geminis would be rendered mute. They are rarely overweight, as they run off nervous energy and tend to under-eat or burn calories at a rate of knots. They find it hard to be still, and there is something bird-like in their quick, restless movements and bright, inquisitive eyes that reflect a busy brain, ceaselessly computing information. Youthfulness is a hallmark of this sign and often shows in their dress sense, too. Look for checks, stripes, or a riot of contrasting colors and styles.

THE GEMINI NATURE

Gemini's archetype is the eternal youth. In physical terms, they tend to look younger than their years, naturally or through artifice, but very often it is the former. Their approach is playful, sometimes irreverent, as they refuse to take life or authority too seriously. Their sense of fun shows in a quick wit, a slapstick sense of humor, and a childlike enthusiasm. Geminis thrive on company and conversation, and, with their butterfly minds, can flit from subject to subject, rarely lost for words.

The sign of the Twins has a Jekyll and Hyde reputation that is unjustified and misleading. Just because they can be changeable does not mean that they have a split personality; think multifaceted rather than two-faced, and

look for the "doubling up" twin symbolism, such as two jobs, two cars, two dogs, two marriages, and an inability to buy or own just one of anything.

LOVE AND RELATIONSHIPS

Geminis may at first be attracted to the person who listens to them, but having someone hang on their every word is not their idea of a relationship. Love talk, or any kind of talk, for a Gemini is most definitely a dialogue rather than a monologue. This sign needs a meeting of minds: someone to play verbal volleyball with, someone who challenges them, will

IN A NUTSHELL

multitasking
animated
talkative
inventive
resourceful
mischievous

KEY PHRASE

"I speak"

work and play with them, but will always hold their attention and understand their complexities.

Commitment is not always easy for a Gemini, as they are such free spirits. The moment they sense any danger of being cornered, they simply slide away, so a long string of affairs until they meet "the one" is not unusual. However, it is also in their nature to "go along" with things, so the other typical scenario is to make an early first marriage that they then quickly grow out of, unless the relationship itself is one that evolves with them. Usually, a second, later marriage is more successful. They are secretly sentimental under that sometimes glib exterior, and can blossom with the emotional stability of the right partner.

VOCATION

Ruled by Mercury, the winged messenger of the gods, Gemini presides over everything connected to the communication industry—marketing, journalism and reporting, television or radio broadcasting and presenting. Geminis are naturals when it comes to spreading the news, since they think incredibly fast on their feet and are talented at using the written or spoken word. This sign also rules driving and professions such as bus or cab drivers.

Geminis are often called the "jack-of-all-trades and master of none," which, up to a point, is true. This does not mean that they are incapable of excelling in their chosen career, but that they need the mental stimulus of variety. They are natural multitaskers, automatically doing more than one thing at a time, mentally and physically. Their hands can be busy with one job while their brain is engaged with something entirely different.

As the Peter Pan of the zodiac, there is also something elusive about this sign. A Gemini client insists that he made it to marketing director not through talent or any particular focus, but by "ducking and diving" his way up the career ladder. The duplicity of this sign knows that language conceals as well as reveals; they are clever and crafty, for good or ill, and can talk their way out of any corner.

TEXTBOOK GEMINIANS

Paul McCartney (b. June 18, 1942), one of the most prolific songwriters and performers of all time, with sales of over 100 million albums and 100 million singles, with the Beatles and as a solo artist. Seemingly ageless, he has been married three times and has five children.

The irreverent **Joan Rivers** (June 8, 1933—September 4, 2014), who wore the multiple hats of TV personality, actress, comedian, author, and playwright, whose works included self help, humor, fiction, and the autobiographies *Enter Talking* and *Still Talking*. She died as a result of complications during surgery on her vocal cords.

The versatile **Anderson Cooper** (b. June 3, 1967), a journalist, author, talk- and game-show host, self-proclaimed news junkie, and anchor of CNN's live news show *Anderson Cooper 360°*.

HEALTH

Unsurprisingly, Geminis need their downtime. While their mental energy is legendary, it can tip over into hyperactivity, and they do not always notice when their physical energy is running out. When they fail to pace themselves properly, they will be slowed down through accidents or falls that produce broken bones, strains, or injuries mostly to the hands, arms, or shoulders. This sign, along with Mercury, also rules the respiratory system and all conditions or problems related to the chest and lungs.

♋ CANCER
(JUNE 22–JULY 22)

SYMBOL: **The Crab**
RULING PLANET: **The Moon**
ELEMENT AND MODE: **Cardinal Water (feminine)**

SPOT THE CANCER

The only sign ruled by the Moon, the typical Cancerian face tends toward roundness. Many men born under this sign have the classic "Man in the Moon" look, complete with picture-book dimples and a wide smile. In women, even when the other features are long or sharp, there is often still a fullness in the cheeks that creates the circular look. The eyes are luminous with flecks of other colors, including the silvery glint of moonlight, and they telegraph care and sympathy. However, the popular image of Cancerians as shy and retiring wallflowers is far from the truth. While they may be cautious initially, they have a wicked sense of clownish fun. Cancer rules the stomach, so watch for the smile breaking into a real belly laugh that is unbelievably infectious. As with the image of the waning and waxing moon, there is something malleable about their features, and they are natural mimics, too.

THE CANCERIAN NATURE

As the sign of the Crab, a Cancerian's knee-jerk response is evasion, to crab-walk sideways rather than confront head on. This springs from their own sensitivity, the fear of offending or wounding, as they themselves can find challenging types abrasive or intimidating. The dislike of directness is part of their charm and diplomacy but can also tip over into second-guessing, going off at tangents, or protracted going around in circles.

The constantly changing face of the moon also reflects the multifaceted Cancer nature. On a good day, they are funny and affectionate, drawing

others toward them like a magnet and letting everyone know how much they are liked and cared for. On a bad day, they can be downright crabby, withdrawn—into the famous shell—or needy. Those crab claws can also cling to grievances and brood over old hurts. One of the Cancer lessons is to learn how to unhook and let go.

LOVE AND RELATIONSHIPS

The Moon rules our emotional nature, needs, and home life, so Cancerians are especially known for their attachment to family. For good or ill, there is usually an incredibly strong tie to at least one of the

IN A NUTSHELL

indirect
cautious
evasive
sympathetic
instinctive
tenacious

KEY PHRASE
"I secure"

parents. They are protective of their loved ones, but the nurturing instinct often reaches beyond blood ties. Rather than collect a wide circle of acquaintances, it is in the Cancer nature to "adopt" their chosen few, creating an extended family. Nobody can storm the barricades, but once someone is accepted into that inner sanctum, they are usually there for life.

The crab shell hides an extremely soft center that is secretly, or not so secretly, romantic and sentimental. When in love, Cancerians make committed and loyal partners, but need absolute trust and emotional security in order to thrive. Their high levels of receptivity are signs of finely tuned instincts, but, if they feel abandoned or misunderstood, they can be touchy and desperately unhappy. They are not always the most articulate of signs, and a partner who understands this is a top must-have.

VOCATION

Cancerians are compassionate and tend to be natural carers and rescuers. They are frequently found in charity work or the caring professions, such as nursing or looking after the elderly. Jobs related to children also belong to this sign, regardless of whether they personally have the maternal or paternal urge to have their own children.

Cancerians are also surprisingly good business people. They may be cautious, but they are also shrewd and brilliant at maneuvering, and their persistence is second to none. Tenacity is a hallmark of the entrepreneurial type, underlying the total dedication to a cause and the refusal to give up easily. For a Cancerian, this is enriched by a desire to create security for their dependents or to act in some way as a spokesperson for their generation. At some instinctive level, they understand that they are passing on the baton.

HEALTH

As this sign rules the stomach, Cancerians tend to move from their "gut" reactions. This is where they physically register their feelings and responses, to the extent of feeling "sick to the stomach" when wounded by others. Food allergies, acid stomach, IBS, and water retention are common afflictions.

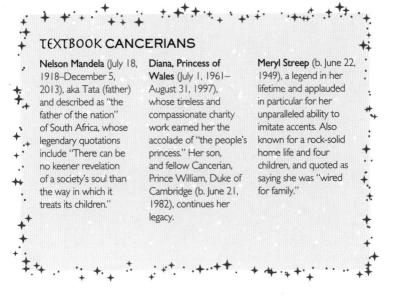

TEXTBOOK CANCERIANS

Nelson Mandela (July 18, 1918–December 5, 2013), aka Tata (father) and described as "the father of the nation" of South Africa, whose legendary quotations include "There can be no keener revelation of a society's soul than the way in which it treats its children."

Diana, Princess of Wales (July 1, 1961–August 31, 1997), whose tireless and compassionate charity work earned her the accolade of "the people's princess." Her son, and fellow Cancerian, Prince William, Duke of Cambridge (b. June 21, 1982), continues her legacy.

Meryl Streep (b. June 22, 1949), a legend in her lifetime and applauded in particular for her unparalleled ability to imitate accents. Also known for a rock-solid home life and four children, and quoted as saying she was "wired for family."

For Cancerians, possibly more than any other sign, there is a powerful link between the emotional and the physical. This sign also rules the breast and the uterus, and if there was a lack of nurturing in the early years, this can leave a very deep wound that is hard to heal. In extreme cases, there is a tendency to internalize pain, resulting in the expression of psychological conflict through somatic symptoms.

♌ LEO
(JULY 23–AUGUST 21)

SYMBOL: **The Lion**
RULING PLANET: **The Sun**
ELEMENT AND MODE: **Fixed Fire (masculine)**

SPOT THE LEO

You only have to think of a full-grown lion to get the Leo picture. Regal, proud, sometimes imposing or magnificent, sometimes just plain cuddly, these individuals are hard to miss, not that they would let you. This sign commands attention, and Leos have a way of announcing themselves. While everyone else may just walk into a room, a typical Leo, consciously or not, makes an entrance and turns heads. Leo rules the back, and you can often spot this sign by their straight spines and excellent posture. Look out, too, for the graceful feline movements, the big-cat profile, the broad face, the Roman nose, and the mane. Many Leos have long, thick, or shaggy hair, and the women generally prefer to be blonde or to "big up" their tresses with highlights. Also look for sun-kissed faces, bright clothing, and statement jewelry.

THE LEO NATURE

As the only sign ruled by the Sun, Leo individuals are to be found at the center of their own universes. They have a knack for being the one around whom all others revolve, and they make wonderful hosts. The Sun rules the monarchy, pomp, and circumstance, and Leos are the kings and queens of the zodiac. They gravitate toward the warmth of good feeling and bask in the rays. Here is the image of the big cat, luxuriating, yawning, and purring, at nobody's beck and call but its own. Some Leos do have a tendency to indolence in this respect, but usually in a contented, relaxed, "don't bother me" way.

You do get the small-cat introverts, but, more typically, a Leo is the one holding center stage, lapping up attention and compliments. They also revel in drama and can easily create one when life gets too tame, but all they really want is to be adored.

LOVE AND RELATIONSHIPS

Leos are often the backbone of their family. They secretly like to think that everything would fall apart if they were not there holding it all together, and, up to a point, they are probably right. They do, however, need to guard against arrogance,

IN A NUTSHELL

creative
proud
warm
self-reliant
efficient
assured

KEY PHRASE
"I create"

bossiness, and interference. They have to learn to bite their lip or look the other way when their fingers itch to take over a job, especially when preserving family relationships and equilibrium.

To be happy in love, their golden rule is never to settle for half measures. The ideal Leo partner is someone who wants to make them the center of their world, someone who makes no secret of their adoration, who is fiercely loyal and lavish with their praise, time, love—and money. Meanness is a Leo's biggest no-no.

Big-hearted, warm, and generous, they will naturally attract a gathering, but genuine friendships are more hard-won. They place enormous value on their personal dignity and find it hard to let the mask slip. Ask them how they are and nine times out of ten they will answer anything from "fine" to "fabulous," no matter what ordeal or hardships they may be going through.

VOCATION

Leos are at their best when they are "Top Cat" and ideally need to be self-employed, the boss, or in a position of responsibility. They are natural born organizers and have their biggest chance of success in a role that allows bold self-expression and creativity. This sign rules jobs connected to the stage, amusements, and gambling, and produces many mesmerizing entertainers and performers.

True, they may have a tendency to take over at the drop of a hat, but they have vision as well as creativity; they can see how something needs to be done, and they take a fierce pride in what they do. The Leo lesson is to allow space for other people's needs, opinions, and egos, as embodied in the opposite sign of Aquarius, sign of the group and objectivity. Leos may learn the hard way that pride goes before a fall, but they have the courage to dust themselves off and start all over again.

HEALTH

Both the Sun and Leo rule the heart and the back. Many Leos will suffer from a back problem of some kind in the course of their lives, especially

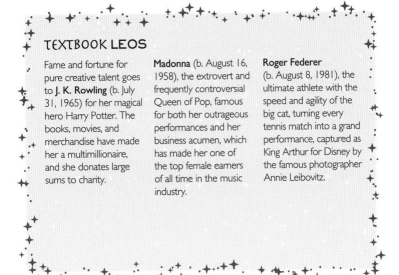

TEXTBOOK LEOS

Fame and fortune for pure creative talent goes to **J. K. Rowling** (b. July 31, 1965) for her magical hero Harry Potter. The books, movies, and merchandise have made her a multimillionaire, and she donates large sums to charity.

Madonna (b. August 16, 1958), the extrovert and frequently controversial Queen of Pop, famous for both her outrageous performances and her business acumen, which has made her one of the top female earners of all time in the music industry.

Roger Federer (b. August 8, 1981), the ultimate athlete with the speed and agility of the big cat, turning every tennis match into a grand performance, captured as King Arthur for Disney by the famous photographer Annie Leibovitz.

when they feel unsupported, unneeded, or unappreciated. This can lead to inertia, depression, or other illness. More than any other sign, Leos thrive and survive on unconditional regard and wither without it. A broken heart or a healthy heart, so much depends on their ability to find personal happiness and contentment. Cholesterol levels are also important for this sign.

♍ VIRGO
(AUGUST 22–SEPTEMBER 23)

SYMBOL: **The Virgin**

RULING PLANET: **Mercury**

ELEMENT AND MODE: **Mutable Earth (feminine)**

SPOT THE VIRGO

Virgos have a reputation for perfectionism, and this often shows in their physical appearance. Designer labels or off the peg, look for the individual who is immaculately put together and who is a triumph of cleanliness and perfect grooming. A typical Virgo would not dream of leaving the house in a hurry, wearing anything stained or in need of repair. Virgo men tend to have square, rugged, yet slightly boyish faces and can be noticeably dapper. The women tend to go to the extremes of immaculate makeup and accessories or the fresh, barefaced look that simply radiates good health. Even if there is scant attention to fashion or adornment, there is a distinct neatness, crispness, or minimalism to the Virgo look. Everything may be slightly understated, but do not be fooled. It can take ages to look this good. Virgos are also the worriers of the zodiac, so look for the pensive expression or the frown.

THE VIRGO NATURE

Many people naturally associate Mercury, planet of language and the mind, with his better-known masculine sign, communicative, live-wire Gemini. Virgo is Mercury's feminine sign, which is expressed through brainpower of a more subtle and exacting kind. Virgo's primary task is to evaluate and analyze. Information, feelings, and decisions are all fed through some kind of mental sieve, separating fact from fiction and isolating essential details. If they ask you a question, which they generally love to do, they will pick apart your answer to find out exactly and precisely what you mean.

Virgo is economical with all resources and can be frugal to the point of extreme self-denial. They can be fanatically tidy and fussy. However, the goody-two-shoes image is frequently a cover for inner turmoil and a wonderfully wacky streak, which most certainly does not tally with the somewhat dry and boring image often ascribed to this sign.

LOVE AND RELATIONSHIPS

There are probably more myths to debunk with this sign than any other. All Virgos are prim and prudish, right? Wrong. In public they may come across as demure, but

IN A NUTSHELL

fastidious
analytical
diligent
dutiful
quirky
astute

KEY PHRASE
"I serve"

behind closed doors they are perfectly capable of raunchiness. This is an earth sign, after all. Are they really critical fusspots? Yes, an insecure Virgo excels at nagging and nit-picking, but usually they would be the first to admit it. They want the best out of their relationship, their partner to be the best that they can be, and to feel safe so that they can relax. Note that this generally does not work the other way around. Virgos are positively allergic to criticism. They will bristle with indignation and feel wounded to the quick.

A Virgo's saving grace is that their highest standards are almost certainly their own, and a partner who understands just how hard Virgos can be on themselves is a must-have. A partner who pulls their weight is also crucial.

VOCATION

Virgos have a dutiful streak and this sign is aligned to service, from the armed forces to tradespeople. This is also the sign of skills and crafts, reflecting the Virgo's unparalleled talent for precision and keen eye for detail. They have self-discipline and a strong work ethic, and can easily become workaholics, as they find it pretty much impossible to delegate. Whom else could they trust to do a task to their own staggeringly high standards? So they do have to learn when "good enough" is acceptable, rather than continually striving for perfection. However, job satisfaction for them lies in constantly honing their expertise. This often springs from being afraid to make mistakes, which, as a result, are rare and never repeated.

Thorough and systematic, this sign rules administrative work of all kinds, but a Virgo will excel in any job that demands accuracy. They can also express their mental agility through the written word. This sign rules health, too, so many Virgos are drawn to the medical professions, often specializing in a particular field.

HEALTH

Virgos are generally health-conscious to the extreme, if only because their most common ailment is anxiety. They worry about their health, just as they tend to worry about all sorts of things. They can worry about not

TEXTBOOK VIRGOS

Agatha Christie
(September 15, 1890–
January 12, 1976), whose
ingenious and intricate
"whodunits" earned her
the accolade of the
Queen of crime fiction.
She was also known for
her love of archaeology,
especially the painstaking
work of excavation.

Actor **Colin Firth**
(b. September 10, 1960),
who became an
established pinup after
playing the tall, dark,
and repressed Darcy in
Pride and Prejudice, and
whose performance in
The King's Speech won
him his first Oscar.

Stella McCartney
(b. September 13, 1971),
who honed her craft as
a designer through study
and internships, and is
described as having
"a signature style of
sharp tailoring and sexy
femininity." As a lifelong
vegetarian, she uses
no leather or fur in
her creations.

having anything to worry about. At their most fretful, Virgos become
cranky, withdrawn, or ill.

In the physical body Virgo rules the pancreas and intestines, so fear,
stress, or imbalances are most likely to manifest in intestinal or assimilation
problems. They are prone to food allergies and are usually suited to a diet
specifically tailored to their sensitive system.

♎ LIBRA
(SEPTEMBER 24–OCTOBER 23)

SYMBOL: **The Scales**
RULING PLANET: **Venus**
ELEMENT AND MODE: **Cardinal Air (masculine)**

SPOT THE LIBRA

Venus' first sign is Taurus, who embodies the earthy, sensual nature of this planet; her second is Libra, the sign of the Scales. The obvious themes of balance and symmetry often show in the physical appearance and, as Venus rules beauty itself, many Librans are real good-lookers. The chief characteristics are well-proportioned faces, a full, sensual mouth, a seductive smile, and sometimes dimples. The eyes are usually large and almond-shaped. Librans are natural socialites, but they can find the role of social butterfly tiring or superficial. You are more likely to find them engaged in earnest, one-to-one conversations. Librans also have an eye for fashion. Casual or dressed up to the nines, their look is stylish and perfectly coordinated.

THE LIBRA NATURE

The constant weighing of the scales lies at the root of Libra's reputation for dithering and indecision. When you have a conversation that is peppered with "on the other hand," "all things considered," "to be fair," and "what do you think?" you will know you are talking to a Libra. As with all the air signs, they love to chat, but they especially love to bounce their thoughts and ideas off others and collect different views and opinions.

The famous Scales also symbolize the two sides to a partnership, and most Librans are natural diplomats. They have huge amounts of charm, and their powers of negotiation and compromise are second to none. On a good day, they are sweetness and light personified. However, when

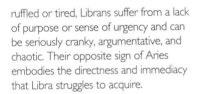

ruffled or tired, Librans suffer from a lack of purpose or sense of urgency and can be seriously cranky, argumentative, and chaotic. Their opposite sign of Aries embodies the directness and immediacy that Libra struggles to acquire.

LOVE AND RELATIONSHIPS

Relationships are of course important for everyone, but for a Libran they amount to life support. A one-sided set of scales is of no use to anyone, so Librans are wired for partnership and generally dislike doing things solo. Loneliness can be their biggest fear, sometimes to the extent of spending

IN A NUTSHELL

sociable
charming
indecisive
diplomatic
discursive
fair

KEY PHRASE
"I relate"

time with people whom they do not especially like. Conversely, they may find themselves saddled with difficult people because they find it so hard to say no and dread giving offence. They are the ultimate people pleasers or rescuers. However, they have a shy streak and often find it hard to ask for what they want in return.

Unsurprisingly, it is rare for a Libran to be without a relationship for any great length of time. The next partner seems to materialize with surprising ease, much to the chagrin of their single friends. They make it look very easy. The flip side of the coin is the "someone is better than no one" trap, over-dependency or neediness, but ultimately they value mental chemistry. Of all the signs, they are the most likely to make a success of a platonic relationship, especially if there is a meeting of minds and enjoyable companionship.

VOCATION

As one of the Venus-ruled signs, many Librans are found in the beauty industry, while others are fashion designers and jewelry experts. If you want to revamp your wardrobe, enlist a Libran. Apart from the fact that they love to be needed and take pleasure in helping you, they have a natural feel for style and fabrics. This is where their indecisive streak disappears. They have very definite tastes, and they know what suits them—and you. This talent extends to interior design, and a typical Libra home will be a place of great beauty, comfort, and luxury.

Libra's sociable nature and ability to charm and soothe can also lead to great success in the diplomatic and business worlds. In addition to a taste for the high life, they excel at wining, dining, and PR. The fair-minded nature of this sign also lends them to legal careers.

HEALTH

Libra rules the kidneys. With their love of good living, Librans need to flush out the old and keep their lives moving. Illnesses may arise from over-indulgence or inactivity, or the inertia of depression. They invariably have a sweet tooth and need to control their sugar intake to ward off the

Actress **Gwyneth Paltrow** (b. September 27, 1972), named by *People* magazine in April 2013 as "Most Beautiful Woman." She announced her separation from husband Chris Martin as "conscious uncoupling," the practice of ending a marriage in a cooperative and respectful way.

Television and music entrepreneur **Simon Cowell** (b. October 7, 1959), best known for his role as talent judge on *The X Factor* and *Britain's Got Talent* series, and for the fact that his entourage includes several of his ex-partners.

One of the original pinups and best-known sex symbols of the 1950s and 1960s, French actress, singer, and model **Brigitte Bardot** (b. September 28, 1934), was considered to be the ultimate in feminine beauty.

risk of diabetes. They tend to have extremely sensitive blood sugar levels and their energy can plummet without regular fuel.

Find me a Libran who does not love a bath. This is where they soak away the tensions of each day and quiet the noise in their busy heads. Librans have to learn firm boundaries to protect themselves from other people's stress and not feel guilty about it.

♏ SCORPIO
(OCTOBER 24–NOVEMBER 22)

SYMBOL: **The Scorpion**
RULING PLANET: **Mars** CO-RULER: **Pluto**
ELEMENT AND MODE: **Fixed Water (feminine)**

SPOT THE SCORPIO

Scorpios exude powerful charisma, but this goes hand in hand with being mysterious and secretive. As the sign of fixed water, either they are the "still waters run deep" type, bewitching but unfathomable, with dark brown or nearly black eyes, or they present the frozen, glacial front, often with startling light or ice-blue eyes. Many Scorpio women have that "ice-maiden" type of beauty. Both types and both sexes are expert at their poker face. In the rare moments that you catch them off-guard, you will notice that the Scorpio eyes are piercing, even hypnotic. Many exude a sultry sexuality and favor the color black. In social situations they tend not to take the lead, preferring to observe and test the water first. Initial impressions are of someone restrained, thoughtful, private, and unreadable.

THE SCORPIO NATURE

Even if a Scorpio comes across as easygoing or flippant, do not be fooled. Emotional intensity is the hallmark of this sign. You can often sense hidden depths and an iron will behind the mask, and when they fix you with that intense, probing gaze, you may feel slightly uncomfortable. If you feel as if your every word is being analyzed, it is because it is. A Scorpio loves to find out what makes you tick, but at first it's a one-way street. It takes time to get to know a Scorpio to the extent of being allowed into their private world in return.

What about that famous scorpion's sting in the tail? There is a vengeful side to this sign, but it is usually saved for when their jealousy is inflamed or

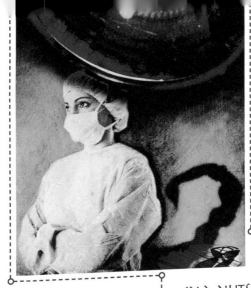

when they feel deeply wronged. The whole gamut of feelings, from love to hate, runs deep, and they can be fiercely loyal or unforgiving with equal purple passion.

LOVE AND RELATIONSHIPS

Scorpio rules the whole cycle of life and death, hence the connection to regeneration and procreation, and in the search for a mate they are not beneath exploiting their sex appeal to the full.

Scorpios take everything seriously and their love life is no exception. They may be capable of strings of affairs, but, when it comes to genuine commitment, they are

IN A NUTSHELL

determined
forceful
thorough
intense
passionate
resourceful

KEY PHRASE

"I regenerate"

the least likely sign to settle for anything less than the real deal. The same applies to friendships, and they are more likely to have a few select and very close soul mates than a wide circle of superficial acquaintances. They would rather stay single than marry someone they cannot love completely. This is fortuitous, as the wrong relationship for Scorpios can be the source of utter misery. Conversely, any kind of unhappiness or rejection can trigger their own capability of becoming destructive, controlling, or cruel.

VOCATION

Traditionally ruled by Mars, planet of action and war, this sign is forceful and determined. Scorpios get a massive kick out of achievement. Tell them that something cannot be done and they will be the first to set out to prove that it can. This may sound supremely competitive, but Scorpios are often more in competition with themselves than with anyone else. Scorpios are at their best when doing a job they feel passionate about, but they do not thrive when constrained by rules and regulations, particularly those that are designed to keep them in the position of humble employee.

Scorpio's redemption is to be found in the nature of their co-ruler, Pluto, commonly referred to as the planet of transformation. Scorpios embody this through their endurance and survival skills. It is not uncommon for a Scorpio to end one way of life, walking away and starting again, and often more than once. They are not unduly attached to the material world, although they are quite capable of amassing wealth, because money is power.

As god of the underworld, Pluto also links Scorpio to the realms of the unconscious and death. Psychoanalysis, detective work, healing, and psychic practices all belong to this sign, as does the work of surgeons, forensic scientists, hospice workers, bereavement counselors, and undertakers.

HEALTH

Scorpio rules elimination and all bodily outlets, the reproductive system and sexual organs, and all illnesses or afflictions associated with these parts of the body. Promiscuity is problematic, because of their susceptibility to

TEXTBOOK SCORPIOS

Harvard University dropout and entrepreneur **Bill Gates** (b. October 28, 1955), co-founder of Microsoft, which has made him one of the richest and most influential people in the world. The Bill & Melinda Gates Foundation donates millions of dollars to charity and research.

Hollywood actress and cool beauty **Grace Kelly** (November 12, 1929–September 14, 1982), who retired from acting at age 26 to embrace a new life of power and prestige as Princess of Monaco. An early and tragic death secured her iconic status.

Surgeon **Christiaan Barnard** (November 8, 1922–September 2, 2001) made medical history when, in 1967, he performed the first human heart transplant, braving unknown territory and transforming the face of life-saving surgery forever.

sexually transmitted diseases, and the emotional vulnerability that they hide so well. Women often struggle with problems related to menstruation, fertility, and menopause.

Stress management is important too. They are prone to taking risks and do not suffer fools gladly. Scorpios have to learn the "live and let live" tolerance of their opposite sign, safety-loving Taurus.

↗ SAGITTARIUS
(NOVEMBER 22–DECEMBER 23)

SYMBOL: **The Archer**
RULING PLANET: **Jupiter**
ELEMENT AND MODE: **Mutable Fire (masculine)**

SPOT THE SAGITTARIUS

Jupiter is Mr. Big of the skies, and it is unusual to find a small Sagittarian—they are usually tall or big-boned. However, even the smaller versions give the impression of boundless energy. Sagittarius rules the hips and thighs, so look for that long, swinging stride. They may remind you of a racehorse, or an exuberant dog, when they bump into you, step on your feet, or knock over your drink. Look for the big smile and the narrow, usually deep-set, quizzical eyes that meet your gaze with a disarming frankness. A quiet Sagittarian is a rarity—most of them are party animals. Listen for the loud voice, ringing laughter, and direct questions. This can come across as rudeness, but Sagittarians tend to wear their hearts on their sleeves and forget that not everyone else does.

THE SAGITTARIAN NATURE

All the fire signs exude an obvious and immediate warmth, but Sagittarians are especially welcoming. They can put even the most uncomfortable person at ease, and expect to be liked, meaning they are puzzled or hurt when they are not. Unfortunately, they can unwittingly create discomfort when their arrows of truth hit the mark with stinging accuracy. They usually dig themselves into an even deeper hole when trying to explain or apologize.

However, there is no malice aforethought. They speak as they find, and they can dish out compliments with the same outspokenness. Their language is peppered with words such as "absolutely" and "totally." They

have an infectious sense of fun and can be hilarious, either in a clownish way or through wit. A typical Sagittarius is also honest and generous.

LOVE AND RELATIONSHIPS

Sagittarians place enormous value on freedom. Marrying too early can be disastrous, as they invariably end up feeling trapped or restricted. Ideally, this sign needs to sow more than the average number of wild oats, and it is not unusual for these freewheeling individuals to go through a long period of promiscuity—and broken hearts on both sides—before

IN A NUTSHELL

intuitive
spontaneous
optimistic
friendly
enthusiastic
ethical

KEY PHRASE
"I seek"

finding the right partner. When they are ready to commit, they do it optimistically, enthusiastically, and with total loyalty. Even so, the best partnerships often have a flavor of the unconventional, as any kind of claustrophobia is a death-knell to their emotional growth and intellectual needs. They will always respect a partner's right to independence, and they are the sign most likely to make a success of a long-distance relationship, or a match with someone from a different culture.

Family may be scattered far and wide, but real closeness tends to be confined to just one or two special relatives. Friendship, on the other hand, is hugely important to them, and typically they have a huge circle of people in whom they invest a great deal of love and energy. An easily jealous partner would therefore not last long, and a true Sagittarian would always choose the single life over the shackles of a controlling relationship.

VOCATION

The love of personal liberty can sometimes lead to a resistance to taking on responsibilities. In the process, however, the thirst for knowledge and meaning will lead restless Sagittarians along all sorts of interesting byways. As the sign of "the higher mind," there is a serious side to their nature; they understand that education takes many forms.

Sagittarius and Jupiter between them have a wide range of vocational concerns. They rule higher education. Many editors, writers, literary agents, and publishers are also born under this sign, as are those in legal professions and work connected to humanitarianism, ethics, and religion. Here we also find the world of athletics and sports, especially equestrianism, as Sagittarius rules horses, being the sign of the centaur.

Jupiter and Sagittarius also rule all things foreign, and many Sagittarians find their niche away from their country of origin. Unsurprisingly, the entrepreneurial spirit is alive and kicking with this big-thinking sign, and they relish the freedom that money can buy. Often there is a certain naivety and childlike trust in the world, which somehow creates luck, albeit invariably at the eleventh hour.

TEXTBOOK SAGITTARIANS

Comedian **Billy Connolly** (b. November 24, 1942) or "The Big Yin" (Scottish dialect for The Big One), whose standup comedy routines are characterized by blue language and outspokenness. After years of serious alcohol abuse, he became teetotal on 30 December 1985.

Actress, singer, and comedienne with a huge personality **Bette Midler** (b. December 1, 1945) was famous for her extrovert, flamboyant, and often outrageous performances.

Explorer, travelogue writer, and novelist **Mark Twain** (November 30, 1845–April 21, 1910), who both made and lost fortunes in his lifetime. However, he always found a way of paying his creditors in full. He cared intensely about human rights and was an ardent supporter of the abolition of slavery.

HEALTH

Sagittarius rules the thighs, including the femur, and the whole pelvic area, including the buttocks and sciatic nerve. They are prone to lower-back injuries that affect these parts of the body. In spite of their athleticism, Sagittarians can be clumsy, too.

This is mostly a robust sign, but with their natural exuberance there is a tendency to go over the top in lifestyle or diet. They are susceptible to weight gain, exhaustion, addictions, or afflictions that arise from excess, primarily liver disease.

♑ CAPRICORN
(DECEMBER 23–JANUARY 20)

SYMBOL: **The Mountain Goat**
RULING PLANET: **Saturn**
ELEMENT AND MODE: **Cardinal Earth (feminine)**

SPOT THE CAPRICORN

Saturn rules all that is large, solid, slow-moving, and enduring. Along with the fact that this is the sign of the hardy mountain goat, many Capricorns have strong frames, which can be either skinny and wiry or heavy-set. This sign and Saturn between them rule the skeleton, and most Capricorns have an excellent bone structure, particularly the cheekbones, giving them striking, unusual, and often highly photogenic faces. Often the face is also noticeably wide. The hair tends to be on the thin side, even when there is plenty of it, and the men often go bald relatively early in life. Young Capricorns look older than their years, but this also works the other way around.

THE CAPRICORN NATURE

Saturn is the planet of age and gravitas, so this sign tends toward seriousness, often as a result of having to grow up quickly. Learning to take responsibility for themselves, and others, is often the hallmark of Capricorns' tough start in life. Among my Capricorn clients we find the woman who was raised by deaf parents and who was the family spokeswoman as soon as she could speak, and the man whose childhood memories included taking himself to the doctor at the age of eight as a way of bypassing his mother's histrionics.

Yet, in spite of their reputation for being cautious rule followers, they are not always glum and gloomy. Once Capricorns break through their own reserve, they can be charming, deeply attentive, and devastatingly funny,

often as a result of learning to use humor as a defense mechanism.

LOVE AND RELATIONSHIPS

A typical Capricorn prefers to build relationships carefully and gradually, rather than assuming intimacy too quickly. They observe other people's boundaries along with their own, quietly gauging reactions and responses as they get the measure of new people or new territory. They like to know where they stand, and also place enormous value on their personal dignity. The danger of rejection or embarrassment is especially sensitive for this sign.

IN A NUTSHELL

reserved
serious
industrious
focused
pragmatic
courteous

KEY PHRASE
"I master"

Emotional risk taking is a big challenge, and it can take a long time for a Capricorn to commit. The fear of intimacy can make them hold back even when they secretly long for wild romance. They tend either to hide behind polite conversation or, again, use humor to create and maintain distance. Their ideal partner is someone who is not fooled by this, or someone who is not cowed by their sometimes authoritative manner. The partner who knows how to find the child within the Capricorn—and bring it out to play—has a playmate and lover for life.

VOCATION

The mountain goat is purposeful and surefooted, able to pick its way up even the craggiest of rock faces. This reflects the legendary Capricorn ambition, but in reality their deeply ingrained work ethic takes many different forms. Not all Capricorns want to run their own company. More accurately, Capricorns are goal-orientated and love to have their plans mapped out clearly and realistically, and to know why they are doing whatever they are doing. Whether it is doing the grocery shopping or building an empire, there is always a clear objective.

As Saturn rules all structures, including hierarchy, and is the planet of work, effort, and respectability, many Capricorns are nevertheless to be found in top managerial posts, government office, or at the helm of their own businesses. They are talented at taking sentiment out of the picture and are motivated by results. This sign also rules mining, building, and architecture, but whatever the profession, the aim is always to build, achieve, and secure. Many Capricorns also find success in later life as they start reclaiming the missed opportunities of their youth.

HEALTH

The built-for-endurance Capricorn has stamina and a great deal of resilience. They tend not to suffer unduly from bugs and are generally blessed with a brilliant immune system. Even when they are ill, they tend to bear their aches and pains with stoicism. However, everyone has their vulnerable spots, and for Capricorn it is the bones, especially the knees.

TEXTBOOK CAPRICORNS

Greek shipping magnate **Aristotle Onassis** (January 20, 1906– March 15, 1975) was the ultimate empire builder. A childhood of riches to rags, owing to his prestigious family becoming refugees, did not stop him from making his first million by the age of 25.

In addition to their own "make good" streak, Capricorn women are often attracted to partners in prestigious roles. **Catherine Middleton**, the Duchess of Cambridge (b. January 9, 1982), clearly made a love match but also married into a lifetime of rules, duty, and service.

Actor, comedian, and producer **Jim Carrey** (b. January 17, 1962) worked full-time rather than finishing high school to help his family through financial hardship and to care for his chronically ill mother. The child in him is the hallmark of his work.

Capricorn is linked to the process of hardening, so also rules the teeth, hair, nails, and cell walls. The correct calcium intake is crucial for this sign. As Saturn symbolizes boundaries, this planet and Capricorn also both rule the skin, the boundary of the physical body. Painful and difficult-to-treat afflictions such as osteoporosis, arthritis, eczema, and psoriasis all belong to the Saturn-Capricorn domain.

♒ AQUARIUS
(JANUARY 21–FEBRUARY 19)

SYMBOL: **The Water Bearer**
RULING PLANET: **Saturn** CO-RULER: **Uranus**
ELEMENT AND MODE: **Fixed Air (masculine)**

SPOT THE AQUARIUS

As two very different planets rule this sign between them, so are there two distinct types of Aquarian. The Saturn type is conservative and tends to dress down, even for a special occasion. Favorite items get worn until they drop into holes, and the women tend to eschew makeup and jewelry. The Uranus type is the opposite, experimenting with styles and colors, regardless of what may be in fashion. They take pride in their own unique look, and often stand out in a crowd. In the physical body, Aquarius rules the lower leg and ankles, and the women, in particular, tend to have long legs and slender ankles. Aquarius also rules the circulation, and this sign usually suffers from the cold. Look for the person huddled in a sweater on a warm day. Also look for stunning eyes, often a piercing metallic blue in Uranian types.

THE AQUARIUS NATURE

Much can be learned about the Sun signs by considering the nature of opposites. The blazing fire sign of Leo prizes individuality, but Aquarius is the voice of the collective. The immediate paradox with this sign is that, although they are the sign of the group, they often struggle to "fit in." It is unusual to find an Aquarian who has not had the experience of feeling deeply "different" from their peers, even from a very early age.

Quirky, curious, and usually of above average intelligence, an Aquarian tends to make sense of the world through logic rather than feelings. Organized, compulsive list makers, placing great value on their own

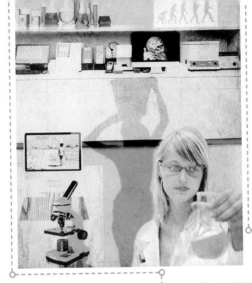

particular way of doing things, these individuals have strong and often unshakeable convictions. As the Aquarian astrologer and one of my first teachers, the late Derek Appleby, once said to me, "Virgos think they are right, Aquarians know they are right!"

LOVE AND RELATIONSHIPS

The textbooks tell us that Aquarians are cold, detached, and lacking in empathy. While it is true that they can give this impression, and some Aquarians end up closing down a lot of their feelings, you can rest assured that more usually there is a

IN A NUTSHELL

systematic
impartial
inquisitive
friendly
humane
original

KEY PHRASE

"I understand"

turmoil bubbling behind the cool mask of indifference. Some of the most emotional people I have ever known are Aquarians.

The journey from friendliness to true intimacy is a long one for this complex sign. Saturnian types, in particular, are easily embarrassed or uncomfortable with displays of emotion and can be disconnected from their own authentic feelings. They crave union yet they create distance, often by giving out the wrong signals of superiority, inflexibility, or militant independence. Uranian types are more gregarious, attaching huge importance to their many and varied friendships.

Unsurprisingly, then, Aquarians need time to build trust and understanding, and successful partnership tends to spring from friendship first. Even when a relationship breaks up, Aquarians tend to keep ex-lovers and partners as friends whenever possible.

VOCATION

Aquarius is objective and stands for the bigger picture of society and the planet. Inside every Aquarian is a conscience, a sense of definite right and wrong, a rebel, or a philanthropist, so any work that is aimed at the greater good has their name all over it. The Aquarian low-on-drama streak works most effectively on causes that need brain power rather than purely an emotional reaction.

Many Aquarians are also to be found in political office, social work, or teaching roles, especially those linked to minorities or special needs. With their appreciation of structure, they are also able administrators, making good team players or leaders within large departments. With Uranus' link to technology, many Aquarians are drawn to the world of IT and inventions. Thanks to their curiosity and being ahead of their time, this is where we find the mad professor archetype, producing geniuses, scientists, and original thinkers.

HEALTH

Aquarius rules the legs, and all accidents or afflictions affecting these parts of the body. It also rules circulation of the blood, and this sign often suffers

TEXTBOOK AQUARIANS

Oprah Winfrey (b. January 29, 1954), who shot to fame by revolutionizing the talk show format through her emotional involvement with her guests. Known as the greatest black philanthropist in American history, she is said to have donated about $400 million to educational causes.

When **Rosa Parks** (February 4, 1913–October 24, 2005) refused, on December 1, 1955, to give up her bus seat to a white person, she became an international symbol for the fight against racial segregation.

The groundbreaking naturalist **Charles Darwin** (February 12, 1809–April 19, 1882) changed the face of evolutionary theory forever. His personal life was subjected to the same systematic detachment—he created two lists entitled "To Marry" and " Not to Marry."

from the cold or circulatory problems. Metaphorically, this links to Aquarians' reputation for coolness and can signal the need to create warmth and passion in their lives.

Regular exercise benefits this sign. With their intellect, there is a risk of living too much in their heads and neglecting the body. Psychotherapy and counseling in any form are also powerful tools for channeling their busy brains along the neural pathways to good mental health.

♓ PISCES
(FEBRUARY 20–MARCH 20)

SYMBOL: **The Fish**
RULING PLANET: **Jupiter** CO-RULER: **Neptune**
ELEMENT AND MODE: **Mutable Water (feminine)**

SPOT THE PISCES

The typical Piscean bears a striking facial resemblance to their symbol, the fish. Note the wide, full-cheeked faces that usually run to fleshiness. Look for the generous, full-lipped mouth, and dreamy, glinting eyes set wide apart that are often doe-eyed and sometimes protruding. Those same eyes easily brim with tears at sad stories or hurtful comments. Often, there is something ethereal about Pisces, either in their beauty or in the way that they move, giving the impression of being disconnected from their physical body. This sign rules the feet, and they often have a distinctive walk.

Sea colors are favorites, and the style is often bohemian or romantic rather than conventional.

THE PISCES NATURE

As the sign of mutable water and co-ruled by Neptune, god of the sea, so is the Piscean nature free-flowing. It is rare to find a Pisces of the seriously shy and retiring kind beyond childhood. They are often larger than life and hugely charismatic, both in social and work scenarios. Both sexes tend to follow their instincts and "go with the flow," and usually have a horror of being confined or controlled.

There is a raw vulnerability to this sign. Their fellow water signs—the Scorpion with its sting and the Crab with its shell and pincers—have their attack and defense mechanisms, but the Fish has no protection other than to wriggle away and swim faster than anyone else. In this respect, Pisceans can be elusive, evasive, indirect, insincere, or paranoid.

Like water, Pisces will take the shape of the vessel, easily or unconsciously fitting into other people's molds and expectations. Finding their own firm sense of self is possibly their biggest challenge.

LOVE AND RELATIONSHIPS

Sensitive, imaginative, sympathetic on one hand, wounded, distrustful, and suspicious on the other, the arena of personal intimacy can be an emotional minefield for this multifaceted sign. Relationships are usually built with a great deal of testing the water before taking the plunge and revealing their innermost persona.

IN A NUTSHELL

sensitive
empathic
artistic
addictive
instinctive
visionary

KEY PHRASE

"I redeem"

Pisceans are natural rescuers, and will do anything for you. They are also great at getting you to do things for them, in a subtle way that is not immediately obvious. There is usually a manipulative streak that they have to learn not to exploit to avoid sabotaging the building of the authentic relationships that they need.

The attraction to those who suffer can unfortunately lead to all kinds of relationship disasters. Often their own need to be rescued is projected on to others. In romance they are far more likely to find happiness with someone with bags of common sense, who can provide emotional security and be their rock in life.

VOCATION

Dreamy Pisceans often struggle with the realities of day-to-day life. They have to figure out how to satisfy their creative appetites as well as pay the bills. Once they find their way upstream, they can achieve great things, but until this turn is made, they can only splash around in the shallows. It is vital for Pisceans, therefore, to find their true vocation. Although they are highly adaptable, the grind of the average, soulless nine-to-five can make them depressed or ill. Usually they are born with a natural gift, something innate that could never be taught.

Inside every Pisces is a thespian struggling to get out. An astounding number of theatre workers, musicians, writers, artists, and poets are also born under this sign.

Pisces' connection to compassion and sacrifice shows in work connected to charities and places of confinement, such as refuges, hospitals, or prisons. Bars, the liquor trade, and all marine work also belong to this sign.

HEALTH

Pisces is the sign of escapism. This can take the form of meditation or mysticism, but Pisceans are especially at risk of alcoholism or substance abuse. Like the other exuberant Jupiter sign of Sagittarius, they find it hard to hit the brake pedal, but Sagittarians tend to do this in the spirit of joie de vivre, whereas Pisceans are more likely to drown their sorrows. The

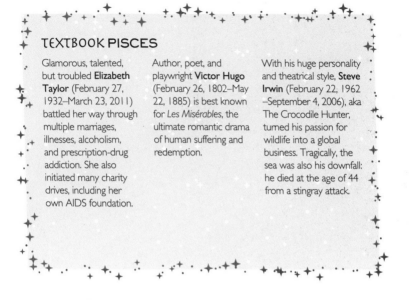

TEXTBOOK PISCES

Glamorous, talented, but troubled **Elizabeth Taylor** (February 27, 1932–March 23, 2011) battled her way through multiple marriages, illnesses, alcoholism, and prescription-drug addiction. She also initiated many charity drives, including her own AIDS foundation.

Author, poet, and playwright **Victor Hugo** (February 26, 1802–May 22, 1885) is best known for Les Misérables, the ultimate romantic drama of human suffering and redemption.

With his huge personality and theatrical style, **Steve Irwin** (February 22, 1962 –September 4, 2006), aka The Crocodile Hunter, turned his passion for wildlife into a global business. Tragically, the sea was also his downfall: he died at the age of 44 from a stingray attack.

single most effective health remedy for this sign is to learn how to step out of the victim role.

In the physical body, Pisces rules the lymphatic system and the feet. Apart from injury, problems include ingrown toenails and bunions. Many Piscean women have a love affair with shoes, or hate them, the latter often arising from difficulty in finding anything to fit them properly.

CHAPTER 2
THE PLANETS

Sun signs can be thought-provokingly accurate, but in many ways they are but the tip of the iceberg, the outer layer of the onion. The real depth and complexity of horoscopy start to emerge when we introduce the other planets. The first seven heavenly bodies—the Sun, Moon, Mercury, Venus, Mars, Jupiter, and Saturn—are known as the Personal Planets. They are followed by the outer, much slower-moving planets, Uranus, Neptune, and Pluto. Modern-day astrology now also includes the planet Chiron, which was discovered in 1977.

THE SYMBOLISM
OF THE PLANETS

Every planet has a sign or signs that it rules. These are also known as the planet's sign(s) of **dignity**. The natures of the planet and sign are complementary and work together harmoniously. The opposite sign(s) are the planet's sign of **detriment**, in which the natures of the planet and sign are in conflict and struggle to understand each other. Note that this does not necessarily mean a simple split between "good" and "bad," but rather that there exists some friction or potential for conflict. Every (personal) planet also has a sign in which it is said to be **exalted**, where it is arguably at its strongest placing. The sign opposite the sign of exaltation is the (personal) planet's sign of **fall**, its weakest placing, in which the natures of the planet and sign are mostly a mystery to each other.

Much astrological interpretation in terms of the natal chart (the horoscope) lies in assessing the combination of planets in signs. This works at many levels, but there are two major strands to planetary symbolism:

UNIVERSAL

What the planet stands for at a general level. For example, Mercury rules everything that comes under the umbrella of communication.

PARTICULAR

What the planet symbolizes in any given chart. For example, if you have Mercury in Aries, the nature of communication is fast, direct, and to the point. If you have Mercury in the opposite sign of Libra, the nature of communication is more discursive and seeks opinions.

Crucially, the "particular" also includes other people. The art of horoscopy really starts to open up when we ask not just "what is this planet?" but "who is this planet?" So the horoscope delineates not just personality characteristics but also the nature of our relationships and those who people our world.

The following cameos of the planets through the twelve signs are offered as illustrations as opposed to absolute givens, snapshots of symbolism as seen through my own client work or in the lives of prominent people. As with the Sun signs in the opening chapter, we are primarily considering the nature of the planet in a sign in isolation, rather than in the context of any particular horoscope. Therefore, the characteristics may run very true to type, or they may be modified, for good or ill, depending on the planet's position within the chart and its relationship to the other planets. In these cameos you will come across mentions of the houses of the zodiac, degree-positions, and Ascendants; these finer details make up the next two, deeper, layers of the onion, and are unpeeled and explored at length in Chapter Three.

	Sun	Leo
☉	Moon (see pages 72–78)	Cancer
☽	Mercury (see pages 79–85)	Gemini Virgo
☿	Venus (see pages 86–92)	Taurus Libra
♀	Mars (see pages 93–99)	Aries Scorpio
♂	Jupiter (see pages 100–106)	Sagittarius Pisces
♃	Saturn (see pages 107–113)	Capricorn Aquarius
♄	Uranus (see page 114)	Co-ruler of Aquarius
♅	Neptune (see page 115)	Co-ruler of Pisces
♆	Pluto (see page 116)	Co-ruler of Scorpio
♇	Chiron (see page 117)	Possible co-ruler of Sagittarius
⚷		

Aquarius	Aries	Libra
Capricorn	Taurus	Scorpio
Sagittarius Pisces	Virgo	Pisces
Scorpio Aries	Pisces	Virgo
Libra Taurus	Capricorn	Cancer
Gemini Virgo	Cancer	Capricorn
Cancer Leo	Libra	Aries
Leo	None	None
Virgo	None	None
Taurus	None	None
Gemini	None	None

☽ THE MOON

SIGN OF DIGNITY: **Cancer**

COLORS: **Silver and white**

DAY OF THE WEEK: **Monday**

METAL: **Silver**

In traditional astrology, the Sun is Lord of the Day and the Moon is Lady of the Night, and they are known together as the Luminaries or the Lights. The masculine Sun symbolizes our day world, the essential self, consciousness, and the life force, whereas the feminine Moon symbolizes our night world and the power of the unconscious. She also rules women, mothers and babies, our childhood, and fertility.

The Moon symbolizes our emotions, instincts, needs, and habitual responses, along with our home, as well as early family life. Often she will describe the mother's nature and character, and therefore the kind of mothering and emotional imprinting we received. If you want to understand the feeling nature, to find the little boy or girl within the man or woman, then the Moon is the place to start.

MOON Herbs and Foods

Lunar herbs and foods are cooling, drying, or sleep-inducing. These include cucumber, coriander, moonwort, pumpkin, cabbage, lettuce, and watercress.

♈ MOON IN ARIES

As the first sign of the zodiac and ruled by the action planet Mars, being "top" is what Aries does best. This Moon symbolizes the pioneering nature, the need to lead—and excel.

Aries rules the self, and psychologically this is a young and "self"-ish, "me first" Moon. Its problem side is the child or teenage-ego state, which is preoccupied with its own needs. The self-esteem pendulum swings from an egotistical sense of personal entitlement to a deeply ingrained and powerful self-belief. When the balance is found and the Aries fire is channeled into true autonomy, the full power of this Moon's awesome single-mindedness comes into its own.

IN A NUTSHELL **efficient, impatient, assured**

♉ MOON IN TAURUS (EXALTATION)

With the Moon's 28-day cycle and connection to women, conception, and nurturing, it makes symbolic sense to find that she is exalted in the fixed and fertile earth sign of Taurus. Here, all the lunar sensitivity and changeability is held, contained, and nourished. Individuals with this Moon often have strong family roots and a deep connection with one or both parents. As a result, they, in turn, tend to take to parenting in a natural and hands-on way. The emotional nature is generally contented and not given to drama. They have a great deal of perseverance and do not mind getting their hands dirty.

IN A NUTSHELL **sensual, secure, down-to-earth**

♊ MOON IN GEMINI

The Moon in Mercury's masculine sign bestows liveliness and quickness, often expressed by a childlike or impish quality, a sense of fun, and slapstick humor. Being big kids themselves, they have a natural understanding of children and how to enter into a child's world. Note the mobility to the features and a lack of self-consciousness that is part of playing the fool, mimicry, and an "up for anything" attitude.

The link to language often shows through rapid speech, a penchant for writing or media work, or cleverness with words. Look, too, for the Gemini duality. The duality may show in early upbringing, such as two homes or two sets of parents. This is also one of the archetypes of the womanizer or the person who leads a double life. This Moon definitely needs stimulus and variety. Often, there is a wide and eclectic circle of friends and a larger than usual repertoire of outside interests.

IN A NUTSHELL **curious, adaptable, mischievous**

♋ MOON IN CANCER (DIGNITY)

The Moon is at home in Cancer, sign of family, parenting, and homemaking. Cancer's concerns of procreation and protection dovetail with the lunar qualities of nurturing, caring, and containing. However, this does not mean that all Cancer-Moon people automatically have an easy or secure start in life. Either early home life can be an emotional idyll, or there is some story of an overly sheltered upbringing or a wounding relationship with one or both parents.

However, whether life started with neglect or with strong family roots and support, these Moon people tend to place enormous value on their own home and have a nurturing streak that will express itself in some obvious way. Either they prove to be natural family makers or they channel their care into fostering, nursing, animals, or a charity.

IN A NUTSHELL **clannish, encouraging, sympathetic**

♌ MOON IN LEO

Every Leo Moon needs its adoring public and special attention. If you are in a relationship with a Leo-Moon person, you can get away with anything, as long as you spoil them and worship the ground on which they walk. The moment they feel as if they are no longer Top Cat, the relationship usually withers and dies.

At work and at home these Moon people are central, competent, and efficient. You can throw pretty much anything at them and, after the initial drama, they will step into their creative mode and find a way to cope. They believe wholeheartedly in their own abilities and, as a result, tend toward bossiness. When it comes to giving orders, they like to be in charge, rather than on the receiving end, and do not take kindly to being told what to do. They loathe being ridiculed and the knee-jerk response to any embarrassment is to stand on their dignity.

IN A NUTSHELL **commanding, affectionate, organized**

♍ MOON IN VIRGO

The Moon in Mercury's feminine sign is more complicated than it seems. Early stories include parents who set impossibly high standards, working parents who never had enough time for their children, and children never feeling good enough or having to win love through achievements. Often they battle with the ingrained belief that they are unlovable, when in fact it was their parents who were unloving.

The Virgo tendency to pick things apart can make the emotional life a hard one, and eating disorders are a common problem. These individuals need gentleness, unwavering approval, and acceptance. They also thrive on routine when it is not too obsessive. Just do not move their things around—they will notice the slightest item out of place—or leave the bathroom in a mess. They may be overly fastidious and fretful but, when happy, they are delightful, witty, and deeply insightful, and when you are in need, they are the first to come to the rescue.

IN A NUTSHELL **vulnerable, meticulous, observant**

♎ MOON IN LIBRA

The Moon in the Venus-ruled sign of the Scales learns about relating from a very early age. Good parenting teaches equality and sharing skills in a home environment that is safe and harmonious, enabling the child to enter adult life with emotional maturity and healthy self-esteem. These qualities are exceptionally important for this Moon as "the other"—the other side of the Scales—is a primary need. The opposite experience, when a child learns that others always come first, can have disastrous consequences, fostering enfeebling dependency and a "someone is better than no one" approach to their love life. When these Moon people turn into serial daters, it flags up the real issue of needing some single time in order to discover their own true sense of self.

Libra's link to beauty and fashion is also important, and these individuals need to feel relaxed in their home or office and happy with their looks, clothes, and accessories.

IN A NUTSHELL **unassertive, peaceable, adaptable**

♏ MOON IN SCORPIO (FALL)

Note that Mars thrives in Scorpio where the Moon is at her most vulnerable. Then throw in the fact that Scorpio is also co-ruled by all-or-nothing Pluto, planet of power, sex, death, and rebirth, and you begin to have a taste of what Moon-in-Scorpio people are up against. Formative experiences among my own clients include early bereavement, the wicked stepmother, being rigidly controlled, and suffering abuse.

These Moon people absolutely have to find their own power or, in return, they can abuse or self-destruct. Often this means rebellion or flying in the face of convention in order to embark upon the healing journey.

A psychologically and spiritually enriched life is possibly this Moon's paramount need. The gift of deep insight often extends into psychic abilities, too.

IN A NUTSHELL **wounded, resilient, transformational**

♐ MOON IN SAGITTARIUS

The Moon in Jupiter's masculine sign is immediately friendly. With a natural clownish streak, they are hugely entertaining company and can break the ice at the most stilted of occasions.

Truth is a big issue for this Moon but, unlike the Sun Sagittarian, they do not always pursue it at the cost of all else. The knee-jerk reaction of steering clear of anything "heavy" can make them shy away from deep truths about themselves, their partners, or their upbringing. They would rather not admit that their mother fell hopelessly short of noticing their real needs. When the inevitable crisis arrives, usually in later life, they wake up to the fact that happiness is inextricably linked with self-awareness.

Emigrating, periods of living abroad, or, especially for the men, living with a foreign partner are also common stories for this Moon.

IN A NUTSHELL engaging, spirited, unbiased

♑ MOON IN CAPRICORN (DETRIMENT)

Note that any Moon-Saturn combination is tricky, as signaled by their conflicting signs of dignity and detriment:

+ The Moon is dignified in Cancer, Saturn's sign of detriment.
+ The Moon is in detriment in Capricorn, Saturn's sign of dignity.

It is not always easy to connect with the real person behind this Moon. On the surface, they are charm personified, and they listen intently. It is only when the conversation is over that you realize that they have volunteered virtually nothing personal. Feelings are markedly compartmentalized and some doors remain firmly closed and locked, even to themselves.

This Moon often signals some early situation that forced them to grow up too quickly, placing the individual at a distinct disadvantage with regard to acquiring intimacy skills. Choosing an older person as a life partner, especially the men, is a common occurrence for this Moon.

IN A NUTSHELL private, honorable, self-reliant

♒ MOON IN AQUARIUS

The Moon in Saturn's masculine sign, with innovative Uranus as co-ruler, is a mixed bag. The Saturn type is objective and sometimes distant. The Uranus type is more avant-garde, with progressive ideas about relationships. Both types are not sure whether they should have feelings at all. They tend to over-rationalize or minimize their emotional needs and, consequently, those of others. Early upbringing experiences are often about parenting that provides the basic needs for survival but goes no further. The best-case early scenario for this Moon is one of parents who practice equality and fairness and who are their child's best friends.

In spite of Aquarius being the sign of groups, these individuals often struggle with shyness and feeling different. In love, their biggest challenge is to heal the split between relationship theory and practice. However, as confidence grows, they usually find happiness when the focus is on a true meeting of minds.

IN A NUTSHELL **brisk, brilliant, humane**

♓ MOON IN PISCES

All the water signs operate on their feelings, but the Moon in Jupiter's feminine sign is possibly the most sensitive combination of all. These individuals are easily wounded, and often there is a difficult start in life connected to themes of suffering, sacrifice, or loss.

Co-ruled by Neptune, god of the boundless seas, these Moon people in fact need firm and clear boundaries. Without them, life is painful and characterized by escapism. Their demons are despondency, self-pity, or paranoia. In love they idealize and can feel overwhelmingly crushed when the loved one topples off their pedestal. They may have missed out on a healthy "separation" phase in childhood, which results in problems with where they stop and other people begin. At best, there is pronounced artistic talent, generosity, and a phenomenal ability to empathize.

IN A NUTSHELL **receptive, impressionable, kind**

☿ MERCURY

SIGNS OF DIGNITY: Gemini and Virgo

COLOR: All that is mixed or multicolored

DAY OF THE WEEK: Wednesday

METAL: Quicksilver

Mercury is Hermes, winged messenger of the gods, and thus he rules communication and everything related to the spoken or written word. Phones, computers, e-mails and all other correspondence, the media, books, diaries, and information in all its guises are Mercury's realm. He is our voice and our words, not just what we say, but the way we say it and how we sound.

As planet of the mind, he governs our thought processes, too, including ideas, opinions, attitudes, and beliefs. He rules youth and early learning, so he has a say in how our outlook and world view are shaped and influenced in our formative years.

Mercury rules the hands and dexterity, and is therefore the archetype of the magician or trickster and thief.

MERCURY Herbs and Foods

Carrots, celery, mushrooms, myrtle, parsley, dill, fennel, and lavender. Peppermint, rich in menthol with soothing and antibacterial properties, also belongs to Mercury, as does the mildly sedative valerian.

♈ MERCURY IN ARIES

This Mercury, in speed-freak Mars' sign, thinks in straight lines and gets to the point. Speech is quick-fire and incisive. These individuals much prefer action to deliberation, and they are brilliant at simply getting things done with no messing around. They thrive on immediacy, and other people's ineptitude or prevarication can drive them crazy.

The downside is impatience, snap decisions that are not properly thought out, or difficulty entering into debate. "Oh, you mean there are other opinions?" Even if they listen politely, they tend to drive down the "my way or no way" street. Their instant solution-finding nature is a godsend in a crisis, but not so hot in the arena of personal relationships.

IN A NUTSHELL **opinionated, direct, witty**

♉ MERCURY IN TAURUS

Mercury in Venus' feminine sign communicates carefully. Individuals with this placing have often had some kind of restriction in their upbringing that is linked to finding their own voice. Battling shyness or body-image issues, feeling like a misfit, and over-protective or unimaginative parenting are all possible factors. At worst, there is muteness, as a result of a family practice of ignoring emotional issues or the "seen but not heard" type of childhood.

In spite of early difficulties, however, they generally adopt a common-sense approach to life. Mercury in Taurus likes to see things in black and white. Maturity brings charm, and they are more likely to play down a drama than to exaggerate it. They are good at finding their niche and resist that which makes them feel unsafe.

As Taurus rules the throat, a distinctive, earthy voice is also a common feature.

IN A NUTSHELL **stoical, pragmatic, tactful**

♊ MERCURY IN GEMINI (DIGNITY)

Mercury and the air sign of Gemini rule everything to do with communication and the function of the mind. The talk-talk planet in the sign of the Twins is therefore the perfect double act. This Mercury loves nothing better than to talk, and speech is quick, animated, amusing, and often excitable. Here we find the hyperactive nature, or the ultimate butterfly mind, effortlessly hopping from subject to subject, or the socially skilled person who can talk to anyone about anything. Skill with language can also show in being bilingual or even multilingual. Sometimes there is a fickleness, but this is often in response to being controlled. This Mercury thrives on diversity and, like air itself, needs to circulate.

Talent with the written word is also a feature, and this placing is extremely common in the horoscopes of novelists, journalists, and prolific songwriters.

IN A NUTSHELL **vivacious, clever, creative**

♋ MERCURY IN CANCER

Mercury in the Moon's sign is usually something of a closed book. This is a water sign, known for being introspective, cautious, and indirect. The mode of expression, even when outwardly extrovert and entertaining, actually gives away very little. These individuals tend to keep their own counsel or confide only in family or friends whose discretion is beyond question. As with the Sun in this sign, the crab shell is a suit of armor, designed to hide vulnerability and to provide a safe haven of withdrawal, and there is usually an intense dislike or fear of confrontation. This Mercury's need for emotional privacy can all too easily outweigh the need to voice their true opinions.

The real strength of this Mercury lies in the ability to care and counsel. They have a rare talent for true listening without interjecting with their own story. The flip side is a tendency to cling to grievances or old beliefs, or to resist change.

IN A NUTSHELL **secretive, evasive, compassionate**

♌ MERCURY IN LEO

Mercury in the Sun's sign is bold, bright, and self-assured. Speech is firm, clear, and sometimes loud. Here we find extrovert and highly expressive performers. They have the ability to put across a message that is aimed at the collective, but which strikes at the heart of every individual. This is the archetype of the speech-maker. Even when the inner nature is humble, they know how to capture a crowd.

However, Leo's link to self-importance signals that this Mercury can be pompous, brilliant at making statements and announcements, but not so skilled at the heart-to-heart stuff of personal relationships. They have to learn that it is not a partner's job to take up the role of audience. Pride can also make it hard for them to admit to being wrong. They crave praise and validation, so being appreciated brings out the best in this Mercury sign; when they love you, their adoration knows no bounds.

IN A NUTSHELL **charismatic, demanding, persuasive**

♍ MERCURY IN VIRGO (DIGNITY & EXALTATION)

Most people associate Mercury with Gemini, his masculine sign, but here is his lesser-known strength, the feminine earth sign of diligent Virgo. The planet of the mind in the sign of discrimination is an awesome combination—insightful, precise, and observant. These individuals put two and two together and always make four. If something does not add up, they want to know why and will not rest until they find out. They would never be so brash as to ask direct or impertinent questions, but the polite smile masks a brain that is working at the speed of light. Their power of analysis is second to none.

Speech tends to be measured, economical, but not necessarily slow. Yes, these Mercury people can be pedantic perfectionists, and guilty of snap judgments, but there is also a quick understanding. Typically, these individuals are highly articulate and deeply interested in the finer details. This is a wonderful placing for a serious novelist or researcher.

IN A NUTSHELL **critical, incisive, accurate**

♎ MERCURY IN LIBRA

The communication planet in the air sign of the Scales speaks in measured, mellow, and often beautiful tones. Here is the born talker and, for that reason, they do not do well being alone. Give the Mercury-in-Libra person someone to talk to, rather than to talk at, and they are happy.

This Mercury carefully weighs up words and thoughts, so at best this is the diplomat, brilliant at seeing all sides to an issue and appreciating everyone's point of view. They loathe confrontation and are the ultimate smoothers and soothers. At worst, it is the hopeless procrastinator. Libra is known for indecision and, with Mercury in this sign, reaching the point of understanding or action can be a tortuous and confusing process. Only when they have made a decision that they are able to stick to, or when a decision is made for them, can they be at peace—until the next dilemma.

IN A NUTSHELL **conciliatory, passive, sociable**

♏ MERCURY IN SCORPIO

Mercury in Mars' feminine sign of intense and secretive Scorpio is, as with the opposite sign of Taurus, associated with silence. Early experiences often carry the hallmark of repression in which speaking freely is forbidden, discouraged, or frightening. These individuals are incredibly deep-thinking but have to learn how to communicate authentically rather than clam up or resort to the classic sting-in-the-tail type of sarcasm. They can be too critical or controlling of others until they learn to subject their own nature and behavior to the same scrutiny. Self-awareness is vital for this placing.

How we do or do not speak about Scorpio's taboo subjects, with sex at the top of the list, is Mercury's domain. Writing about sex is perfect symbolism for this Mercury.

With Scorpio's link to both healing and death, this Mercury is the "talking cure," the archetype for the sex therapist, bereavement counselor, and all types of psychoanalysis. Mediums and psychics are found here, too.

IN A NUTSHELL **reserved, bewitching, insightful**

MERCURY IN SAGITTARIUS (DETRIMENT)

In traditional astrology, Mercury is the planet of the so-called lower mind, which rules our early learning and concerns itself with the minutiae. Mercury in Jupiter's signs—planet of the so-called higher mind, which rules adult learning, our philosophy, and the bigger picture—is therefore something of a mismatch.

Mercury's voice in fiery Sagittarius is fast and exuberant, and speaks as it finds. These individuals therefore have a reputation for tactlessness. However, the idea of being deliberately hurtful is alien to them. They learn to tone it down when they realize that others find them overwhelming or even insulting. They often struggle with putting their feelings into words, but with time, this Mercury placing can be eloquent and scholarly. Beliefs run deep, but the attitude is cheerful and optimistic rather than overly serious. There is also often an aptitude for learning foreign languages.

Being honest to a fault is part of their truth-freak nature. Honesty and justice are exceptionally important, and they cannot bear to be disbelieved.

IN A NUTSHELL **forthright, visionary, intellectual**

MERCURY IN CAPRICORN

Mercury expressed through Saturn's feminine sign is controlled, authoritative, and understated. The speaking voice can be rather monotonous, although not without resonance.

Guardedness in this Mercury can take the form of quiet reserve, answers that are not really answers, or deadpan humor, all of which are effective deflectors for too much intimacy. In extremis, this Mercury can close down. If they do not want to talk about something, no amount of pleading or threats will make the slightest difference. Only when they are ready to talk do you have a hope of finding out what the problem is.

On a good day, however, these individuals are delightful companions, even if they take life too seriously. Here we find weighty authors and respected actors who take on serious roles.

IN A NUTSHELL **courteous, strict, constructive**

♒ MERCURY IN AQUARIUS

There is a line of thought in modern astrology that considers Aquarius as Mercury's sign of exaltation, although traditional astrology gives this as Virgo. Either way, Mercury expressed through Saturn's masculine sign is a powerful placing. Innovative Uranus as co-ruler, and Aquarius belonging to air—element of the mind—adds up to individuals of above-average intelligence or who have an unusual take on life.

In personal relationships, too much head and not enough heart can make this Mercury dispassionate, aloof, or dismissive. Even if they start their sentences with, "I may be wrong but…," they secretly believe that they are right. If you want to convince them otherwise, you need all the facts and figures at your fingertips. Sentiment has little place in their world, and emotional scenes can leave them indifferent or distinctly uncomfortable.

The saving grace with these Mercury people is that they are interesting —and interested. Thriving on conversation and debate, they are often controversial and admire the same quality of "being different" in others.

IN A NUTSHELL **matter-of-fact, methodical, quirky**

♓ MERCURY IN PISCES (DETRIMENT & FALL)

Mercury in Jupiter's feminine sign can be a fish out of water. We all know what it is like to try and "reason" with someone "in love." Like oil and water, the two simply do not mix. With Neptune, god of the sea, as co-ruler, this Mercury is at the mercy of feelings and thoughts that are free-flowing, boundless, staggeringly deep, and teeming with undercurrents. These individuals often have early experiences of emotional hardship, in which their feelings were disregarded or minimized.

Making sense of emotional matters may be a tall order, but this struggle often produces exceptional poets, singers, and songwriters. What they cannot say easily, they express through rhyme and song.

The tricky side to this detrimented Mercury is distortion of the truth, from white lies to outright deception.

IN A NUTSHELL **vulnerable, emotional, empathic**

♀ VENUS

SIGNS OF DIGNITY: Taurus and Libra

COLOR: Green

DAY OF THE WEEK: Friday

METAL: Copper

Venus is Aphrodite, goddess of love, and known as the lesser benefic. Your Venus sign tells you about your relating skills, what you are looking for, and how you approach relationships. She is feminine and rules women, all pleasure seeking, lovemaking, beauty, art, music, and the fashion industry. She also rules sustenance, everything from food to the money we make in order to live.

In a man's chart, regardless of sexual orientation, she often describes the kind of partner he attracts or to whom he is attracted.

VENUS Herbs and Foods
Anything sweet, delectable, and more-ish. Chocolate is definitely Venusian, and many Venus types have a sweet tooth. Venus' produce is fragrant or delicious, such as jasmine, apple blossom, all roses, and all soft fruits. Venus also rules thyme, lavender, geranium, vanilla, and any herbs that calm over-indulgence in food.

♈ VENUS IN ARIES (DETRIMENT)

Venus is in dignity in Libra, sign of partnership, and therefore is said to be in detriment in the opposite sign of independent Aries. This does not mean that all Venus-in-Aries individuals are doomed to failure in romance, but their task is not an easy one. Ruled by Mars, they are feisty and egotistical, and have strong opinions. They have to learn that partnership needs consultation and negotiation.

Venus people often experienced a troubled adolescence in which they lacked healthy role models, which in turn tends to arrest the development of relating skills.

They may go through long periods of being single, but when they do set out to find a mate, they waste no time. If they like you, they will head straight for you every time they see you. However, they need fast results or they will just move on to their next conquest.

IN A NUTSHELL **direct, impulsive, impatient**

♉ VENUS IN TAURUS (DIGNITY)

Venus in feminine, earthy Taurus is soft, sensual, and tactile. These Venus people thrive on physical contact, although they do have to feel comfortable with you first. This is a safety-conscious sign, but, with emotional security in place, this Venus placing wins hands down when it comes to kisses and cuddles.

These Venus people tend not to rush into love unless they are young. The older they get, the more they deliberate, and the more they will choose reliability and solvency—they love retail therapy—over physical attraction. The flip side to this Venus is complacency. They would be the first to admit to a lazy streak and dislike of change. They may either miss or ignore the early-warning signs of love trouble.

As with Mercury in Taurus, the sign that rules the throat, this Venus often denotes the beautiful voice.

IN A NUTSHELL **affectionate, possessive, charming**

♊ VENUS IN GEMINI

Venus in Mercury's masculine sign is sociable, talkative, and breezy. Their feelings can change rapidly, not through insincerity, but because their boredom threshold is low, so they can also be flighty or fickle. As Gemini is the sign of the Twins, they are quite capable of having two relationships simultaneously. They are the arch-flirters and keep their options open, inevitably giving out mixed messages in the process. Understanding their own needs and sexuality may lie at the heart of contradictory behavior.

Eventually, however, sexual or commitment issues are usually resolved, choices are made, and this Venus placing indicates at least two major relationships in the course of a lifetime.

These Venus people need someone to talk to. In love, they make playful partners as long as heart and head are both engaged. They are best suited to someone who is quick-witted and who knows how to keep them on their toes.

IN A NUTSHELL **mercurial, amusing, amiable**

♋ VENUS IN CANCER

Venus in the Moon's sign is caring and fiercely protective toward loved ones. In relationships they are primarily drawn to those who are homemakers and who want children, but sometimes these Venus people can be so fused with their own family that they seem to need no other. Many of them remain single, diverting their care into other outlets, such as their work, home, charity, and close friendships.

This Venus is cautious and often shy, so it is rare for them to get hooked into anything destructive. They are turned on by gentleness and a sympathetic nature. Loudness or aggression is a big turn-off. They are wonderful at looking after you, although the women must guard against becoming "mother" instead of "lover." Needy behavior, never throwing anything away, and saving money are their security blankets, but what these Venus people really need is to be cocooned in love.

IN A NUTSHELL **loyal, dependable, appreciative**

♌ VENUS IN LEO

Venus in the Sun's sign is big-hearted, warm, and vibrant. These individuals are usually incredibly generous in the giving of love, and their appetite for receiving it is even bigger. They aim to impress, and a diet of attention, admiration, and adoration is an inexhaustible feast for this Venus.

When mature and secure, even if they privately yearn for more themselves, these Venus people will dish out the same glorious validation to others, too. However, rejection or embarrassment is their biggest dread, so they usually will not show their own feelings until they are sure of yours. They are also unlikely to seek a mate who is "beneath" them. This Venus can be haughty and wants someone to be proud of.

IN A NUTSHELL **regal, passionate, demonstrative**

♍ VENUS IN VIRGO (FALL)

Virgo's analysis and precision reach their full potential through Mercury, planet of the mind, but these same qualities can be passion killers for Venus. Whether thinking it or saying it out loud, these Venus people tend to pick apart their loved ones' behavior, choices, and so on. However, criticism is rarely the conscious intention. The challenge of Venus in Mercury's sign is to practice tolerance.

Venus in her sign of fall suggests that these individuals should all be celibates or not blessed with beauty, but this textbook interpretation is not the reality. Indeed, Venus in Virgo oozes a particular brand of sex appeal. The look is well-groomed and beautifully assembled. Similarly, flirting is not overt. They have their own definite partner criteria, usually including good health and a strong work ethic. Their reputation for frugality is debatable. Their wardrobe may be minimalist or stuffed with designer labels, some never worn, still with price tags on.

IN A NUTSHELL **choosy, curious, subtle**

♎ VENUS IN LIBRA (DIGNITY)

Venus teaches us all about relating, and she is therefore powerful in the sign of the Scales, the symbol of partnership. There is absolutely nothing that one half can do without affecting the other. These Venus people simply need their other half to be there; they are inextricably linked, and make heaven-sent partners, although they can tip over into too much neediness. They have conventional ideas about togetherness, so, unsurprisingly, affairs or long-distance relationships have a short shelf life. They admire beauty and sophistication, and more often than not their partner is a good-looker, but ultimately they seek someone who is easygoing, relaxing to be with, and equally invested in "The Relationship."

Even this dignified Venus, however, suffers from the notorious Libran balancing act of indecision.

IN A NUTSHELL **attentive, artistic, compliant**

♏ VENUS IN SCORPIO (DETRIMENT)

Venus in Mars' feminine sign is intense and deeply emotional, although you would be forgiven for not thinking so on first impression. Co-ruled by Pluto, there is a secretive streak and a need to stay in control of their feelings. This belies a passionate nature, and they may even come across as cold or indifferent. Often there is some disturbing experience in their early life that taught them to give away nothing. Having suffered from powerlessness, they instinctively or consciously protect their vulnerability.

These Venus individuals usually ooze sex appeal and mystery, and look drop-dead gorgeous in black. They admire strength and bravery. Passivity bores them. They are prone to jealousy or possessiveness, but, when secure or truly put to the test, they make awesome partners. Their all-or-nothing nature means that they can commit better than anyone.

Venus in Scorpio has a highly developed sixth sense and can also symbolize the psychic or the healer.

IN A NUTSHELL **impervious, powerful, alluring**

♐ VENUS IN SAGITTARIUS

Venus in Jupiter's masculine sign does not play games, and when they give their heart away, which they do easily, total belief in their loved ones follows automatically. They are naive in this respect, and often go through a few disappointments before learning that love does need common sense as well as faith. When unhappy, they can be prone to promiscuity, but their innate optimism enables them to bounce back.

Freedom is a big issue. They do not equate needing space with a lack of commitment, and being with a partner who wants to be joined at the hip is usually a claustrophobic disaster. They can do unconventional relationships as long as the trust is there. A partner with good financial skills helps, as their own approach to money can be rather unrealistic.

Being attracted to someone from another culture as a life partner, especially in the case of men, is a common occurrence for this Venus.

IN A NUTSHELL **honest, trusting, unrestrained**

♑ VENUS IN CAPRICORN

Venus in Saturn's feminine sign takes all affairs of the heart seriously. These individuals generally seek a partner who is hard-working, cares about material security, and will be there for the long haul. Innate caution, often springing from a strict or restricted upbringing, keeps them from jumping into any relationship too quickly.

These Venus people are known for their endurance, sense of responsibility, and pragmatism. They are perfectly capable of passionate attractions, but the choice of a life partner can be treated with the same sang-froid as the choice of a house or job.

As so often with this sign, these individuals can sometimes seem aloof or older than their years. They usually learn early on about restraint, respectfulness, and duty. Capricorn rules structure and tradition, so this Venus also symbolizes the necessity for a "professional" partner who will take his or her place in the hierarchy.

IN A NUTSHELL **steadfast, formal, assiduous**

♒ VENUS IN AQUARIUS

Venus in Saturn's masculine sign is an enigma. There is a double-sided nature to Aquarius that can be described as the conventional (Saturn) versus the unconventional (Uranus). This split also shows when expressed through the other planets and especially through Venus. Here we come up against the strait-laced, repressed, or asexual nature, or the person who is into wild experimentation. Both types struggle to connect with their authentic feelings and often find it hard to express themselves with passion, even when they privately feel very strongly.

The most successful relationships for these Venus people are those that spring from friendship. They admire brains and ideas, and are especially drawn to a mate who shares both their intellectual interests and their social scene. Unhappiness is usually the result of overriding compatibility issues. They are quick to recover from disappointment, however, and tend to keep ex-partners as friends.

IN A NUTSHELL **broadminded, unusual, convivial**

♓ VENUS IN PISCES (EXALTATION)

Venus in Jupiter's feminine sign is compassionate and imaginative. These individuals are the ultimate romantics, and they can be blissfully happy if they find their soul mate. However, they are also extremely vulnerable, and, more usually, the quest for love brings many emotional highs and lows. Their feelings are easily crushed, and the art of self-protection does not come readily. Co-ruled by Neptune, their feelings can be positively oceanic, and personal boundaries are a struggle. They are driven by the urge to merge, but are secretive when insecure. Escapism can blossom into huge creative achievement when it is channeled into the arts, but the other extreme is to anesthetize pain through alcohol or drugs.

Empathy entwined with a self-sacrificing streak also picks out this Venus as an archetype of the rescuer. These Venus people fare best with partners who are kind yet not over-indulgent, with their own strong sense of self.

IN A NUTSHELL **idealistic, gentle, receptive**

♂ MARS

SIGNS OF DIGNITY: **Aries and Scorpio**

COLOR: **Red**

DAY OF THE WEEK: **Tuesday**

METAL: **Iron**

In traditional astrology, Venus is feminine and rules women; Mars is masculine and rules men. Together they are the love planets, Venus in terms of pleasure and relating skills, Mars in terms of pursuit, lust, and libido. Mars in a woman's chart, regardless of sexual orientation, often describes the kind of partner she attracts or to whom she is attracted.

Mars is the god of war and symbolizes everything to do with how we go into battle and how we handle the cut and thrust of life. Psychologically, he symbolizes heated emotions and he rules anger, passion, and pain.

MARS Herbs and Foods
All that is sharp, stinging, pungent, hot, and spicy, including garlic, ginger, onion, nettles, thistles, horseradish, pepper, paprika, and cayenne. Rocket, considered to be an aphrodisiac, also belongs to Mars.

♈ MARS IN ARIES (DIGNITY)

Mars in the dynamic and positive fire sign of Aries is just where he wants to be. The sense of immediacy and urgency of these speedy individuals is second to none. They are usually at the front of the queue when help is needed, particularly for the underdog. With their ability to cut through red tape, fearless campaigning is one of the hallmarks of this winning combination. Human rights are especially close to their hearts.

Mars in Aries is proactive (plans ahead) as opposed to reactive (deals with it when it happens). These guys spend their lives constantly anticipating all possible scenarios, troubleshooting, and working out a plan of attack. They are fiercely independent, do not suffer fools gladly, and can channel anger into their beliefs.

Love is boring unless it is a challenge. This Mars thrives on the thrill of the chase and needs a partner who can keep their attention.

IN A NUTSHELL **egotistical, immediate, proactive**

♉ MARS IN TAURUS (DETRIMENT)

Taurus is slow and sensual, comfortably at home with Venus, but can punch and bellow when expressed through Mars. Alternatively, the Mars-Taurus combination signals inertia, the couch potato, or the nature that is peaceable until provoked. Physically, this Mars has the constitution of an ox but is something of a plodder and hates to be rushed. Results are won through stubborn perseverance or the "I'll prove you wrong" kind of determination.

This placing is often associated with brutality and bullies. It is the stuff of hard knocks and can signify early experiences of abuse, especially in a woman's chart.

IN A NUTSHELL **deliberate, blunt, enduring**

II MARS IN GEMINI

If you want to pick a fight with a Mars-Gemini person, have your dictionary at the ready. Mars in Mercury's sign is incisive and highly articulate. Here are the warlords of words and the masters of verbal volleyball. Conversely, words as weapons can show as sarcasm, the throw-away lines of thoughtlessness, wounding intentionally or unintentionally, or the hatchet journalist, pursuing any line of enquiry just to get that story.

Mars in the double sign of the Twins can also signal the individual who is multi-talented or who holds down two jobs. They are generally not perfectionists and can make quick work of tasks that others would find time-consuming. Typically, they run off nervous energy, have countless ideas, and spend a lot of time on the phone. They can talk anyone into anything or themselves out of any tight corner. As Mars symbolizes men, women often have two significant relationships or marriages.

IN A NUTSHELL quick, inventive, versatile

MARS IN CANCER (FALL)

Any Mars-Moon combination is tricky, as signaled by their conflicting signs of dignity/exaltation (strength) and detriment/fall (weakness):

+ The Moon is dignified in Cancer, Mars' sign of fall, and is in detriment in Capricorn, Mars' sign of exaltation.
+ Mars is dignified in Scorpio, the Moon's sign of fall, and is in detriment in Taurus, the Moon's sign of exaltation.

Mars prefers to move in straight lines, but Cancer is depicted by the sideways-moving crab. Mars is direct and pointed, Cancer is cautious, inward-looking, and avoidant. They want to be needed, but at the first sign of trouble, pain, or rejection, Mars-in-Cancer individuals will retreat into their shell, keeping hurt inside, or employ passive-aggressive tactics.

Their sensitivity is such that their mood can change quickly and with little warning. They also fear giving offence. They will go all around the houses, test the water, and need others to read between the lines.

IN A NUTSHELL moody, protective, indirect

♌ MARS IN LEO

Mars in the Sun's sign is a royal, commanding, creative, and powerful combination. These individuals have forceful personalities, and their talents are usually expressed in a center-stage way. Their self-belief is wholehearted, but they need others to believe in them, too. They are highly motivated by praise, recognition, and adulation. The Mars-drive coupled with Leo's knack for drawing a crowd creates a showmanship quality, charismatic performers, and "the show must go on" work ethic. In business, this is the archetype of the managing director, the CEO, and the entrepreneur.

Leo correlates to the 5th house of the zodiac (see Chapter Three), in which we find children. I have frequently found this placing to denote an adored and usually artistically talented child. Lovers also belong to the 5th, and these Mars people embody the art of courtship.

IN A NUTSHELL **creative, bossy, big-hearted**

♍ MARS IN VIRGO

Mars in the second of Mercury's signs is the epitome of precision. Here we find the hallmark of pure craftsmanship and the honing of skills. I have seen this placing in the charts of those whose work requires the "cutting edge," such as picture framing or tiling, and in those who have exceptional talents in the worlds of technical drawing, fine art, and intricate design. This Mars is measured, diligent, patient, and painstaking, and the attention to detail is second to none.

In love matters, this placing can be problematic. The red planet can find it hard to sizzle in Virgo, even though, as noted earlier, Virgo's "prim and proper" reputation is misleading. However, the particular combination of Mars in Virgo can signal problems with sexuality or celibacy.

This placing has frequently shown for those whose happiness is thwarted by the quest for non-existent perfection, for celibates, or for those in platonic yet otherwise functioning marriages.

IN A NUTSHELL **picky, fastidious, exacting**

♎ MARS IN LIBRA (DETRIMENT)

Traditional astrology tells us that Mars is weakened by being in Venus' sign. In basic terms this makes sense, as Mars is the god of war and the go-getter, whereas Libra is the sign of negotiation and peace. There is an obvious conflict, but it can simply mean that the fight (Mars) for peace (Libra) is a major concern for these individuals.

In relationships, Mars-in-Libra people have a lot of charm but rely heavily on their partner, often to the extent of feeling aimless and unmotivated when having to do things alone, or feeling like a failure in their (rare) single periods.

These Mars people are social animals and need others to inspire and encourage them, so they tend to under-achieve if left to their own devices for too long. They generally dislike overt confrontation, although they can be last-word freaks, and tend to cloak anger in distaste.

IN A NUTSHELL **likeable, dependent, diplomatic**

♏ MARS IN SCORPIO (DIGNITY)

As with Mars' other sign of dignity, Aries, the hallmarks of this placing are a competitive streak and determination. However, whereas fiery Aries tends to blaze a public trail toward personal excellence, the water sign of Scorpio is more undercover. Here is the archetype of the secret agent or psychoanalyst—and control freak. These individuals have definite ideas about how things should be done, and they do not like to be contradicted or overruled. Anger tends to take the shape of inward fuming: the more serious their rage, the more deadly their revenge.

Mars in Scorpio takes time to fathom. A calm and dignified exterior, donned especially with new people in new situations, conceals a deep-feeling nature. Underneath the charisma lies a fierce intensity and it is rare for them not to get what they want. Once they learn how to conquer jealousy or control issues, they make amazing partners and, with huge libidos, lovers.

IN A NUTSHELL **controlling, passionate, insightful**

↗ MARS IN SAGITTARIUS

Mars in the fire sign of the Archer is bursting with feverish activity. These individuals tend to approach life with tons of enthusiasm but sometimes find it hard to stay focused. Often their lives are characterized by moves that create the freedom to travel, learn, or explore.

In this respect they are not generally career people, finding it difficult to stay in one job, although they are perfectly capable of reaching the top of their tree once they find the right cause. Neither do they enter into committed relationships easily unless they find a true soul mate. In love they need honesty and a long rein. The paradox is that they are intensely loyal. In anger, they will flare up in an instant, especially if wrongly accused, and they can be hurtful in the heat of the moment, but never bear a grudge.

Another hallmark of this Mars is equestrian sports, such as polo.

IN A NUTSHELL **energetic, friendly, faithful**

♑ MARS IN CAPRICORN (EXALTATION)

Mars in the earth sign of goal-orientated Capricorn is the embodiment of harnessed energy and unwavering purpose. These individuals are incredibly hard-working as they tackle each new project. Their eye is already on the next step upward, and new challenges just make them work even harder. Their phenomenal staying power usually lies at the root of their success and their drive toward material security.

This placing usually signals a great deal of self-control and restraint, such as being uncomfortable with public displays of emotion. Anger stops short of real fireworks, but the black clouds of a seriously bad mood can linger for a long time. This Mars is not lacking in earthy passion, but this is for behind closed doors. Conventional at heart, as opposed to emotional risk takers, they value long-term, lasting relationships, and they like to know exactly where they stand. Often they choose a partner who is older, especially an authority figure or someone who has already "made it."

IN A NUTSHELL **dedicated, purposeful, traditional**

MARS IN AQUARIUS

Mars in the fixed air sign of Aquarius signals a nature that is generally smart, competent, and objective. With their systematic approach, they can shift enormous amounts of work. Often they make great team players, or are good at managing teams, as they are masters of the overview rather than being intent on individual glory. The paradox is that they can be inflexible. Utter personal conviction and high principles can result in a fixed code of ethics from which no one is allowed to deviate. This can create problems when it comes to the give and take of relationships. In love, they can be slow to open up to intimacy, and tend to place friendship and shared intellectual interests over passion.

Overall, when it comes to fighting a cause, this Mars is in a league of his own. These individuals are attracted to partners who are similarly strong-minded and on their own mission.

IN A NUTSHELL **principled, progressive, original**

MARS IN PISCES

Mars in the mutable water sign of Pisces creates two contrasting images: the iridescent fish gracefully flashing through the water, and the slippery fish that is crafty or amoral. The former approaches life in an imaginative or romantic way, the latter deceptively or fearfully. Here we find the con artist, the seducer, or the "poor me" victim, who plays, consciously or unconsciously, on the vulnerabilities of others.

Whether they use their talents for good or ill, these individuals tend to operate on instincts rather than on rationale. At worst, it is others who make the sacrifices; at best, this is a charitable Mars, working their fingers to the bone in order to ease the suffering of those truly in need.

Mars in Pisces is a subtle and complex energy. They dread rejection. Anger can be mistaken for hurt, so these individuals are more likely to cry, sulk, or brood than throw things.

IN A NUTSHELL **hypersensitive, elusive, imaginative**

4 JUPITER

SIGNS OF DIGNITY: Sagittarius and Pisces
COLORS: Purple, deep blues
DAY OF THE WEEK: Thursday
METAL: Tin

Jupiter is the sixth of the personal planets and thus plays a role in the delineation of personality. However, he is notably slower-moving than the other personal planets, changing sign only once every twelve months. Therefore, in order to individualize this planet further, it helps to consider its house position (the sections of the wheel of the horoscope when divided into 12; see Chapter Three), as well as its sign. Hence, for each chart, there are two Jupiter sections to read:

✦ Jupiter by sign
✦ Jupiter by house position, regardless of which sign he is in.

For example, if you have Jupiter in Gemini in the 10th house:

✦ First read Gemini (3rd house) as the primary interpretation
✦ Then read Capricorn (10th house) for extra insight.

In the following snapshots, the qualities may describe the individual's nature and/or may be more recognizable in others, such as family or partners, or in life experiences.

In traditional astrology, Jupiter is known as the greater benefic. His main principle is expansion, and he is the bringer of joy, good fortune, opportunity, higher education, freedom, and travel. He rules all things foreign, both people and places. He is also the planet of truth and humanity, ruling the law, justice, religion, philosophy, and the higher mind. His nature is optimistic, encouraging, and extrovert.

Jupiter herbs are said to be cheering and benevolent. They include red clover, dandelion, asparagus, and sage. Jupiter also rules fertile soil, grapes, raisins, and wine.

♈ JUPITER IN ARIES OR 1ST HOUSE

Jupiter loves the bigger picture, and Aries is matchless in finding the most direct route from A to B. This combination denotes a trailblazing nature and the visionary. The level of self-belief is notably high, and these Jupiter people rarely stop to think whether something is achievable or not. The gap between thought and execution is minimal, and they aim straight for the target, either for their own desires or in the interest of an important cause. For them, second place is for losers.

IN A NUTSHELL **unswerving, dynamic, the entrepreneur**

♉ JUPITER IN TAURUS OR 2ND HOUSE

Jupiter in Venus' feminine sign is materialistic and appetitive, and enjoys the good life. The means to do so can either come from a wealthy family or through being self-made. This is Aristotle Onassis' Jupiter, powerfully placed in his 2nd house of finances. However, Jupiter's entrepreneurial nature is not always free-flowing in this sign of fixed earth. Opportunities can be slow to materialize, or too much family security can kill the hunger that so often characterizes the fulfillment of potential.

IN A NUTSHELL **dependable, comforting, the provider**

♊ JUPITER IN GEMINI (DETRIMENT) OR 3RD HOUSE

Jupiter is said to be weak in Mercury's signs and vice versa, but this does not mean that Jupiter blessings pass by these individuals. However, they may be hard won. Jupiter rules publishing; Harry Potter was rejected by 12 different publishers until J. K. Rowling found lucky 13. The multiplicity of the Twins also signals a series of books rather than a one-off. In my own client work, this Jupiter has shown as two marriages, both to foreigners, and as the achievement of two degrees.

IN A NUTSHELL **breezy, playful, full of ideas**

♋ JUPITER IN CANCER (EXALTATION) OR 4TH HOUSE

Benefic Jupiter in the Moon's sign is the ultimate protector. These Jupiter people usually have a close relationship with one or both parents. In turn, they often find themselves in a markedly caring role, either in their relationships or through vocation. Sometimes their personal freedom is limited as a result.

Cancer's connection to the homeland can also signify patriotism. The dominant feature of Nelson Mandela's horoscope is this Jupiter conjunct Pluto (power and transformation), encapsulating his life's purpose to challenge white supremacy and win human rights for the South African people.

IN A NUTSHELL **loyal, a safe harbor, strong sense of national identity**

♌ JUPITER IN LEO OR 5TH HOUSE

Big, bold Jupiter is at his most creative and most obvious in fiery Leo. This combination is all about the confidence and expression of the individual. These Jupiter people generally have tons of personality and considerable "pulling power" through personal magnetism, the ability to command attention, or artistic talent. Often there is the influence of someone who has absolute belief in them. This is Céline Dion's Jupiter, whose manager and then husband, René Angélil, mortgaged his home to fund her first record.

IN A NUTSHELL **devoted, big-hearted, a sense of occasion**

♍ JUPITER IN VIRGO (DETRIMENT) OR 6TH HOUSE

Expansive Jupiter in picky Virgo can show in fretting over details, the obsessive-compulsive, or too much work and not enough play. With purist Virgo's link to diet and health, here we also find food intolerance or allergies, or the teetotaler. This Jupiter is powerful for those who find their vocation in the health industry or whose life's purpose is bound up in allegiance to others. This is the Jupiter of Burma's Aung San Suu Kyi (b. June 19, 1945), who, over the past two decades, has spent a total of 15 years under house arrest.

IN A NUTSHELL **meticulous, discriminating, efficient**

♎ JUPITER IN LIBRA OR 7TH HOUSE

Jupiter in the sign of the Scales is fair, reasonable, and considerate, finding it easy to be pleasant and impossible to be vindictive. This Jupiter acts for the good of the other and is a blessing for all relationships. This is Roger Federer's Jupiter (b. August 8, 1981), who laid out his priorities in advance of the birth of his second set of twins, saying he would not hesitate to miss any tournament to be with his wife, Mirka. He did just that, pulling out of the Madrid Open Masters.

IN A NUTSHELL **tolerant, diplomatic, popular**

♏ JUPITER IN SCORPIO OR 8TH HOUSE

Jupiter expands whatever he touches. With Scorpio, that means feelings, the good and the bad. There are no indifferent ones. These Jupiter people live life intensely and tend to take huge risks, emotionally or in pursuit of a goal. They can be immensely successful when they follow their passion. Sir Cameron Mackintosh (b. October 17, 1946) knew from the age of eight that his future lay in theater production. Emotional spectacles of power, sex, and death, such as in *Les Misérables*, probably the best-known of his shows, are Jupiter-in-Scorpio personified.

IN A NUTSHELL **X-ray vision, influential, the power to change lives**

♐ JUPITER IN SAGITTARIUS (DIGNITY)
OR 9TH HOUSE

Jupiter's qualities and concerns resonate with Sagittarius, sign of learning, travel, and exploration. These Jupiter people often have a foreign theme of some kind in their lives; they paint on a broad canvas and approach life with enthusiasm, optimism, and a deep sense of trust. They intuitively know that things happen for a reason, which is an effective safeguard against bitterness or cynicism. In crisis, they can make a crucial leap of faith and, in doing so, create their own "luck." They are truth freaks with a pronounced sense of right and wrong.

IN A NUTSHELL sincere, ethical, good-natured

♑ JUPITER IN CAPRICORN (FALL)
OR 10TH HOUSE

Capricorn belongs to Saturn, who symbolizes the opposite principles to Jupiter. This combination is therefore full of conflict and can speak of the struggle between pleasure and duty, freedom and discipline, or the "for your own good" type of miserable upbringing. At worst, this is a blinkered nature that brooks no disobedience or difference. At best, it is the workhorse, the ambitious individual who fights against all the odds, such as Charlie Chaplin (April 16, 1889–December 25, 1977), whose childhood was blighted by hardship and the workhouse.

IN A NUTSHELL conscientious, persevering, humorous

♒ JUPITER IN AQUARIUS OR 11TH HOUSE

Mr. Big—Jupiter in the sign of the collective—sees what is best for most. These Jupiter people are bright, objective, and scientific, approaching life's issues and crossroads with head rather than heart. This is Albert Einstein's (March 14, 1879–April 18, 1955) Jupiter. They like to deal with facts and figures rather than personal agendas, whether their own or other people's. They make natural leaders, managers, or "breaking the mold" politicians, such as Barack Obama. Often they find their blessings through their friendships or peers.

IN A NUTSHELL **principled, revolutionary, a social conscience**

♓ JUPITER IN PISCES (DIGNITY) OR 12TH HOUSE

Jupiter's softer concerns, such as care, compassion, and the spiritual life, are beautifully expressed through sensitive Pisces. These Jupiter people have an enormous capacity for love, although, as so often with this sign, the road to happiness is often paved with suffering or sacrifice. This Jupiter therefore steers many individuals into the caring or artistic professions. Tina Turner (b. November 26, 1939) found her reserves of inner strength and peace through Buddhism, enabling her to escape from the violent marriage to Ike and enjoy a phenomenal professional comeback.

IN A NUTSHELL **philanthropic, selfless, a connection with the mystical**

♄ SATURN

SIGNS OF DIGNITY: Capricorn and Aquarius

COLOR: Gray

DAY OF THE WEEK: Saturday

METAL: Lead

Saturn is the seventh and last of the personal planets. He still plays a role in portraying character, but he is very slow-moving, changing sign only once every two-and-a-half years. The slower the planet, the more it will speak of a backdrop to life rather than just the personal nature. In order to individualize Saturn further, it helps to consider his house position (see Chapter Three) as well as his sign. As with Jupiter, for each chart there are two Saturn sections to read:

+ Saturn by sign
+ Saturn by house position, regardless of which sign he is in.

For example, if you have Saturn in Libra in the 9th house:

+ First read Libra (7th house) as the primary interpretation
+ Then read Sagittarius (9th house) for extra insight.

In the following snapshots, the qualities may describe the individual's nature and/or may be more recognizable in others, such as family or partners, or in life experiences.

In traditional astrology, Saturn is known as the greater malefic. His main principle is contraction—the opposite to Jupiter's expansion. If Jupiter is "yes," then Saturn is "no." He is the bringer of solemnity, restriction, obstacles, boundaries, endings, and ultimately death. Saturn is the enemy of the "Lights" of life, the Sun and Moon, being in detriment in their signs of dignity, Cancer and Leo. He rules authority, career, duty, and responsibility. His nature is pessimistic, realistic, and serious.

SATURN Herbs and Foods

The most important Saturn herb is comfrey, which has bone- and skin-healing properties and encourages cell regeneration. Saturn's foods are bitter or sharp, including spinach and parsnip.

♈ SATURN IN ARIES (FALL) OR 1ST HOUSE

Aries is fiery, dynamic, and ego-centered, energies that are thwarted when expressed through the solidity of Saturn. These Saturn people invariably experience frustration or intense aloneness in situations of new vs. old, self vs. family, or the individual against the system. Courageous convictions are a hallmark of their missions or identity issues. Chaz Bono (b. March 4, 1969), transgender child of Sonny and Cher, has Venus and Saturn at exactly the same degree in this sign, symbolizing the rejection (Saturn) of his feminine (Venus) self (Aries).

IN A NUTSHELL enterprising, self-belief, a refusal to give up

♉ SATURN IN TAURUS OR 2ND HOUSE

Saturn in Venus' feminine sign is mostly down-to-earth with a "no frills" approach. Here we find astute business types, especially in the fields of finance and produce, such as Linda McCartney (September 24, 1941–April 17, 1998). Responsibility for or attitude to money and security is a major issue. At best, this Saturn is the archetype of the benefactor. Early hardship, however, is not uncommon, either through genuine lack or because financial help is withheld; this can signal a family doctrine of "stand on your own two feet," no matter what.

IN A NUTSHELL dependable, constant, the sugar daddy

Ⅱ SATURN IN GEMINI OR 3RD HOUSE

In psychological terms, Saturn is the *senex* (the wise old man), whereas Mercury, ruler of Gemini, is the *puer aeternus/puella aeterna* (the eternal youth). Here we find the old head on young shoulders, or vice versa, but both tend to a youthful outlook. They usually prefer to talk than write, which can be an arduous process, sometimes as a result of difficulties with early schooling. Similarly, a blind spot around paperwork can lie at the root of a general resistance to worldly concerns, such as paying bills on time, if at all.

IN A NUTSHELL **information gatherers, constructive, family longevity**

♋ SATURN IN CANCER (DETRIMENT) OR 4TH HOUSE

With Cancer's connection to early roots, it is not uncommon for these Saturn people to experience a tough start to life, mostly linked to the struggles or even a tragic history of one or both parents. Drew Barrymore's (b. February 22, 1975) mother was born in a Displaced Persons Camp in Germany, while Drew's own childhood was lost to her parents' divorce, stardom, and drug and alcohol abuse, as told in her autobiography *Little Girl Lost*. The transition to adulthood can be a lonely one but often teaches the ability to self-parent.

IN A NUTSHELL **strong survival instincts, understanding burdens of others, the ancestral home**

♌ SATURN IN LEO (DETRIMENT) OR 5TH HOUSE

Leo is hot and glorifies the individual, but Saturn is cold and rules the hierarchy, so this combination is an obvious clash. As in Aries, this combination bears the hallmark of personal limitations vs. the system. This is Bill Clinton's (b. August 19, 1946) Saturn, posited in his 10th house of public life; his efforts to conceal his affair led directly to his impeachment. With Leo's link to children, this Saturn sometimes shows as parental favoritism.

IN A NUTSHELL **authoritative, choosing personal responsibility, fulfillment later in life**

♍ SATURN IN VIRGO OR 6TH HOUSE

Saturn resonates with the earth signs, and this combination is industrious, exacting, and disciplined. These Saturn people like to put their resources of brains, time, and money to good use, so they can also be scrupulously frugal. They are the first to evaluate a job and put their shoulder to the wheel. They usually see the details that others miss. Richard Branson's (b. July 18, 1950) Saturn (empire) in Virgo (Virgin brand name) in his 2nd house (money) symbolizes the business that has made him one of the richest men in the world.

IN A NUTSHELL **conscientious, strong work ethic, the health/business specialist**

♎ SATURN IN LIBRA (EXALTATION) OR 7TH HOUSE

It makes sense that serious Saturn is exalted in Venus' sign. Relationships are the means by which we learn and mature. Many celebrities born under this Saturn are known as much for their partnerships as they are for their individual achievements, such as Prince Rainier III of Monaco (May 31, 1923–April 6, 2005), who was married to Grace Kelly, and Serena Williams (b. September 26, 1981), whose sister and tennis doubles partner is her sister Venus. This Saturn is also the archetype of authority figures at their best, such as the wise judge or the equal rights employer.

IN A NUTSHELL **a strong marriage, fairness, total commitment**

♏ SATURN IN SCORPIO OR 8TH HOUSE

Saturn in the Mars-Pluto sign of fixed water has unparalleled depths of desire, persistence, and resilience. Britain's first female prime minister, Margaret Thatcher (October 13, 1925–April 8, 2013), had this Saturn sitting on her Scorpio Ascendant (self and public face). She was known as "The Iron Lady" and for her famous words, "The lady's not for turning." These Saturn people rarely deviate from their beliefs or routines, and they can move mountains of work almost without anyone else noticing. Often there is a legacy of emotional hardship.

IN A NUTSHELL **fearlessness, phenomenal willpower, turning negatives into positives**

♐ SATURN IN SAGITTARIUS OR 9TH HOUSE

Saturn in Jupiter's masculine sign presents the conflict of two opposing forces or beliefs. Saturn's nature is to restrict and Jupiter's is to learn and liberate, so here we find the serious philosopher, philanthropist, or freedom campaigner, such as Che Guevara (June 14, 1928–October 9, 1967) and Abraham Lincoln (February 12, 1809–April 15, 1865). These Saturn people have to learn how to do battle with authority in life and how to find the middle ground between claiming their own space and their responsibility to others.

IN A NUTSHELL **humanitarian, ethical, barristers and professors**

♑ SATURN IN CAPRICORN (DIGNITY) OR 10TH HOUSE

Saturn in his own sign of Capricorn is purposeful but always calculating. These Saturn people generally have an ambitious streak but know the pitfalls of making a fast buck. There is an empire builder in all strong Saturnian types, but this Saturn, in particular, is surprisingly versatile and can turn his hand to anything, whether it is children's entertainment (Walt Disney, December 5, 1901–December 15, 1966) or running a country (Barack Obama, b. August 4, 1961). The flip side of the coin is rigidity and those who never bend the rules.

IN A NUTSHELL **able, goal-orientated, influential father or role model**

♒ SATURN IN AQUARIUS (DIGNITY) OR 11TH HOUSE

Saturn shares his second sign of dignity with innovative co-ruler Uranus. These Saturn people are therefore either "by the book" operators, or challengers of anything outdated. Both types have groundbreaking potential in their areas of interest. Here we find the objective, supremely logical brilliance of the scientists, social reformers, or computer wizards. This is Garry Kasparov's (b. April 13, 1963) Saturn, former World Chess Champion turned political activist. Their weak points are being blinkered by very strong personal opinions and detachment in personal relationships.

IN A NUTSHELL **systematic, impartial, social conscience**

♓ SATURN IN PISCES OR 12TH HOUSE

Saturn is the reality planet, whereas Pisces is the sign of romance or escapism. Along with the 12th-house themes of loss or self-undoing, this combination adds up to a painful struggle with the demands of a harsh world. These Saturn people often have to realign their dreams with what is actually possible or get entangled in their own nets. Piscean Nick Leeson (b. February 25, 1967), the former derivatives broker, has Saturn at 29 degrees of Pisces, a fixed star called Scheat, which denotes downfall. His staggering losses on the stock market brought about the collapse of Barings Bank, the UK's oldest investment bank, as portrayed in the movie *Rogue Trader.*

IN A NUTSHELL **intense empathy, rescuers of the weak, experiences of redemption**

THE MODERN PLANETS

These three planets are known as the "modern" planets, so called because they were unknown to ancient astronomy. Each is a co-ruler of a particular sign and not a substitute for the traditional ruler. They are also known as the Trans-Saturnians—the planets that come after Saturn—or as the generational planets, as they take many years to travel through each sign. With these slower-moving planets, interpretation tends to rest more heavily on the house position (see Chapter Three).

Evolutionary events at the time of each planet's discovery reflect their symbolic nature. Similarly, people whose horoscopes are stamped by these outer planets often represent the zeitgeist (spirit of their time), bringing the message into the consciousness of the collective and becoming the voice of their generation.

TEXTBOOK EXAMPLE

Spike Milligan (April 16, 1918–February 27, 2002), groundbreaking, irreverent comedian and strident campaigner, addressing both domestic violence and environmental issues, who suffered from bipolar disorder throughout his life. The "signature" of his horoscope is an Aquarius Ascendant, Uranus dignified in Aquarius in the 1st house (self/physical body), and in aspect to both Sun in Aries and Moon in Gemini.

♅ URANUS
CO-RULER: AQUARIUS

Uranus was discovered in 1781, coinciding with the French and American revolutions and the industrial revolution in England. He is therefore the planet of rebellion, anarchy, social advancement, ecology, and technology. Both Bill Gates and the late Steve Jobs have strong Uranus-Aquarius features in their horoscopes.

In mythology, Uranus is the sky god, and he rules all that comes "out of the blue."

He challenges all that Saturn stands for, such as hierarchy and traditional rules, and his nature is innovative, explosive, sudden, unexpected, erratic, or unpredictable.

Typical Uranian types are primarily different. Brilliant, quirky, nervy, eccentric, unstable, a wild child or a genius, a scientist or social misfit, they are always unusual, unconventional, or original in some way.

Uranus is at his most powerful for those individuals who have a Uranian-Aquarian theme to their horoscopes.

♆ NEPTUNE
CO-RULER: PISCES

Neptune was discovered in 1846, coinciding with advancements in photography, film, and pharmaceuticals, notably anesthetics. Gas was replacing oil for lighting, bringing with it streetlights and a nightlife of brightly lit bars. Neptune is therefore the planet of imagination, illusion, glamour, and escapism, from mysticism to the pain-free world of drugs or alcohol.

In mythology, Neptune is god of the sea, and he rules all things marine. Psychologically, his realm is the boundless watery world of the emotions, ruling fusion, suffering, and sacrifice. His nature is subtle, seductive, addictive, mysterious, magical, or disorientating.

Typical Neptunian types are primarily sensitive. They are often artistic, vulnerable, and acutely receptive to other people's feelings and moods, running the gamut from empathy to paranoia.

Neptune is at his most powerful for those individuals who have a Neptunian-Piscean theme to their horoscopes.

TEXTBOOK EXAMPLE

Princess Diana (July 1, 1961–August 31, 1997), Sun in Cancer, Neptune in Scorpio, and Chiron in Pisces, all linked to one another and to Pluto. This reflects the woman who captured the imagination of the world, her emotional wounds, and the empathy that characterized her charity work.

♇ PLUTO
CO-RULER: SCORPIO

Pluto was discovered in 1930, coinciding most notably with the discovery of nuclear power and the rise of psychoanalysis through the work of Freud and Jung, among others. Pluto is thus associated with the latent power of either potential annihilation or transformative healing. He also signifies plutocracy, the wielding of power through wealth.

In mythology, Pluto is the god of the underworld, and he rules all that is hidden, invisible, secret, or taboo. Entering therapy constitutes the exploration of our own underworld, unearthing our buried issues in order to heal. One of his images is the phoenix, the legendary bird of rebirth. His nature is transformative, uncompromising, intense, and extreme.

Typical Plutonic types are primarily powerful. Arguably their strongest gift is that of insight, and many Plutonic types are natural psychologists, sleuths, or healers.

Pluto is at his most powerful for those individuals who have a Plutonic-Scorpio theme to their horoscopes.

TEXTBOOK EXAMPLES

Scorpios **Marie Curie** (November 7, 1867–July 4, 1934), born with a Sun-Pluto aspect, and **Indira Gandhi** (November 19, 1917–October 31, 1984), with a Mars-Pluto aspect, both carried Pluto's masculine power and broke into male-dominated worlds, transforming the way for women of the future.

♃ CHIRON
POSSIBLE SIGNS OF DIGNITY: SAGITTARIUS OR SCORPIO

Chiron was discovered in 1977, coinciding with the rise of the holistic health industry and the subsequent spiraling awareness of the mind, body, and spirit connection. In terms of astrological tradition, Chiron is but an infant without an official sign of dignity, yet he has already found his way into most Ephemerides, the book of tables that tracks the journeys of all the major planets. Chiron is here to stay.

Melanie Reinhart is a recognized Chiron expert and author of *Chiron and the Healing Journey: An Astrological and Psychological Perspective*. Reinhart originally proposed Chiron as co-ruler of Sagittarius, a symbolically appropriate placing for Chiron the Centaur. She has since proposed that a case could be made for Chiron co-ruling Scorpio, sign of healing and magic, but also suggests that, as Centaurs are creatures without dominion, perhaps we do not necessarily need him to rule any particular sign at all.

In her book she explains that his importance lies in how he illuminates issues of awakening—for example, health crises and life-changing experiences, the encounter of guides and teachers, and the recapitulation of previously encountered trauma or insights.

In mythology, Chiron is recognized as the most superior Centaur, standing apart from his unruly brethren. Civilized, knowledgeable, and kind, this skilled physician, teacher, astrologer, and oracle is a fount of ancient wisdom. Ultimately, he is the archetype of the Wounded Healer as, unable to use his healing arts

TEXTBOOK EXAMPLE

Steven Spielberg (b. December 18, 1946), whose movies address the deepest human wounds of war, terrorism, the Holocaust, and the slave trade, has the Moon conjunct Chiron in Scorpio. ("Conjunct" means that the two planets are in conjunction, i.e. positioned next to each other.)

upon himself, Chiron gave up his god-status in order to die and thereby
end the eternal agony of a poisoned arrow wound. The full power of
his message is captured in his "rebirth," being returned to source and
immortalized in the constellation of Centaurus.

   Those with Chiron prominently placed in their horoscopes often take
up the mission for the collective, notably in the role of mankind's healers
or educators whose work is destined to survive them for all time.

THE MOON'S NODES

☊ NORTH MODE   ☋ SOUTH MODE

Every horoscope includes the position of the Moon's Nodes. These are
not heavenly bodies but imaginary points at which the Moon cuts across
the Ecliptic—the celestial sphere that marks the apparent orbit of the Sun.
The Ecliptic takes its name from the fact that eclipses can happen only
when the Moon is on or near this line.

   You will find the position of the Moon's Nodes in their own column in
the Ephemerides. You will find only the North Node listed, as the South
Node is always at exactly the opposite point. For example, if you have
the North Node at 10 degrees of Aries, your South Node will be at
10 degrees of Libra.

   The line of the Nodes is personified as a dragon: The North Node
marks the point where the Moon crosses the Ecliptic from south to north,
known as *Caput Draconis*—the head of the dragon. The North Node is
considered to be fortunate and to symbolize good karma, being where the
dragon feeds and gains nourishment.

   The South Node marks the point where the Moon crosses the Ecliptic
from north to south, known as *Cauda Draconis*—the tail of the dragon. The
South Node is considered to be unfortunate and to symbolize bad karma,
being where the dragon excretes.

The Sun and the Moon (the Lights) symbolize the eyes of the dragon, and the dragon "eating" the Lights refers to the phenomenon of eclipses.

The Moon's Nodes are at their most powerful when acting as a "testimony" to interpretation, underlining a theme that is already in evidence.

For example, Prince Charles' Moon is positioned at 0 degrees of Taurus in his 10th House (the section of the horoscope in which we locate career/public life). His exalted Moon symbolizes the influential women in his life, especially his mother, the Queen, as the Queen's own Sun marries up with this point, also being at 0 degrees of Taurus. This already powerful picture is reinforced by the fact that Prince Charles' Moon is also conjunct the North Node at 5 degrees of Taurus.

⊕ THE PART OF FORTUNE

This is also an imaginary point, which is derived through the mathematical formula of the degree of the Ascendant, plus the degree of the Moon, minus the degree of the Sun. Fortunately, all astrological software does the sums for you. Its name speaks for itself, as it simply picks out a lucky degree in the horoscope and, like the Nodes, often acts as testimony to an astrological theme already in play.

TEXTBOOK EXAMPLE

Victoria Beckham (b. April 17, 1974) started her journey to success with the Spice Girls—Part of Fortune in Gemini conjunct Mars in Gemini, sign of collaboration and the voice in the 11th house, house of groups.

CHAPTER 3
ASCENDANTS
AND THE HOUSES

When we start to make the leap from general astrology to horoscopy—the study of individual charts—we find that the wheel of the horoscope is divided into twelve sections, called the houses, which are a crucial part of astrological interpretation as they provide the context for the planets. In other words, when looking at an actual horoscope, we can immediately see where each planet "lives." The interpretation of any given planet in a sign is now modified and enriched as we determine its particular role in the life of the individual or the "native," the person to whom the natal (birth) chart belongs.

7 8 9 10 11 12

THE ASCENDANT

o - o

WHAT IS IT?

The Ascendant (or rising sign) is not a planet but the sign rising over the eastern horizon at the time of our birth; it marks the beginning of the 1st house (see page 136). This crucial angle can be calculated to exactitude only if the time of birth is known, which is why time is so important to an astrologer. Without a birth time, it is a little like looking at a clock with no hands, so, in essence, the more accurate the birth time, the more accurate the horoscope. (See page 152 to find out how to create a Noon Chart instead, if your time of birth is unknown.)

   All twelve signs of the zodiac rise over the eastern horizon in any 24-hour period. Owing to a phenomenon called Short Ascension or Long Ascension, some signs pass over the horizon more quickly than others, but as a rule of thumb the Ascendant changes sign approximately every two hours.

WHAT DOES IT SYMBOLIZE?

The Ascendant is the face we present to the world, the personality traits we exhibit, and the lens through which we filter all information and experiences. It is the first thing that others see about us or that we see about others. Think of it as the cover of a book. It is not "the whole story," but a flavor of what is to come and an indication of how we come across, how we engage with others, especially in first encounters, and how we approach life in general.

As the angle of the 1st house of the physical body, the Ascendant also has a big say in how we look. As illustrated in Chapter One, all the Sun signs have their own physical characteristics, and these can be replicated when the sign is rising, or when that sign's planet is posited in the 1st house. For example, an Aries Ascendant or Mars in any sign in the 1st house may manifest physically as red hair or sharp features. Physical appearance is summed up as a combination of the characteristics of the Ascendant, Sun sign, Moon sign, and any planet in the 1st house, so the following descriptions will be modified accordingly for each individual.

Similarly, with the Ascendant's link to the physical body, this angle also has to be taken into account for health concerns. Again, these factors originate in the Sun signs and can be replicated through the rising sign.

Regardless of the Sun sign, the ruling planet of any horoscope is the planet that rules the sign on the Ascendant. This planet acts as the native's particular "significator" and is of primary importance in both natal and predictive interpretation. The following descriptions provide an overview of each of the twelve signs when found on the Ascendant. Note that this information is also relevant when the sign's ruling planet is posited in the 1st house, in any sign. For example, a 1st house Mars shares many of the characteristics associated with an Aries Ascendant.

♈ ARIES ASCENDANT
OR MARS IN THE 1ST HOUSE

With an Aries Ascendant, regardless of the Sun sign, the ruling planet of the horoscope is Mars. This planet's sign and house will be a primary consideration in the process of interpretation.

PHYSICAL CHARACTERISTICS Long face and neck, sharply delineated features, often thin-lipped, an aquiline or Roman nose, a pointed or pronounced chin, red hair or red tones to the hair—either natural or added—arched eyebrows, ruddiness in the complexion.

MANNER AND SPEECH Can come across as aggressive, direct, authoritative, or vigorous. The approach to life is generally enthusiastic but impatient, with the focus on action and initiative rather than deliberation. Individuals with this rising sign or a 1st house Mars tend to snap into "how to" solution-finding when faced with a challenge. Language is usually brusque or quick-fire, initially failing to factor in other opinions or practical red lights. Intentions are either self-serving or well-meaning and humane for someone in need of their warrior spirit.

HEALTH Life's demands tend to be handled with powerful bursts of energy, followed by the reaction of exhaustion. Prone to headaches and sinus problems, or injuries to the head or face.

FAMOUS ARIES ASCENDANTS

John Lennon, Bette Midler, Barbra Streisand,
Joan Rivers, Errol Flynn, Kourtney Kardashian

♉ TAURUS ASCENDANT
OR VENUS IN THE 1ST HOUSE

With a Taurus Ascendant, regardless of the Sun sign, the ruling planet of the horoscope is Venus. This planet's sign and house will be a primary consideration in the process of interpretation.

PHYSICAL CHARACTERISTICS Strong or jutting chin, square face, neck variable—either short and wide or long and slender, especially in the women—broad shoulders, a muscular frame, a full, sensuous mouth, often a concave "ski slope" nose, a gracefulness in movement, even if big-framed or overweight.

MANNER AND SPEECH Can come across as pedantic, deliberate, thoughtful, or seductive. The approach to life is cautious with a tendency to hang back, inwardly running a safety check as an initial response to a new person, problem, or situation. Individuals with this rising sign or 1st house Venus generally resist being coerced into any course of action and can therefore be stubborn, but they know what they want and have particular likes or dislikes. In personal relationships they are the masters of patience, reassurance, humor, and kindness, and thrive when receiving the same in return.

HEALTH Usually exceptional stamina. Prone to problems with the throat or thyroid. Often a slow metabolism and a tendency to gain weight easily.

FAMOUS TAURUS ASCENDANTS

Billy Crystal, Serena Williams, Dionne Warwick,
Felipe VI of Spain, Queen Latifah, Humphrey Bogart

Ⅱ GEMINI ASCENDANT OR MERCURY IN THE 1ST HOUSE

With a Gemini Ascendant, regardless of the Sun sign, the ruling planet of the horoscope is Mercury. This planet's sign and house will be a primary consideration in the process of interpretation.

PHYSICAL CHARACTERISTICS Youthful appearance, fidgety or distinctive mannerisms with the movement of the mouth or hands, small, neat features, glittery eyes, usually thin, wiry, or willowy frames.

MANNER AND SPEECH Can come across as nervy, chirpy, flippant, or highly curious. Often, they are animated conversationalists with a childlike sense of fun. Everything is flavored by speed or versatility, whether it is actions, thought processes, or the speaking voice. Individuals with this rising sign or a 1st house Mercury usually have a way with words, including perfect comic or theatrical timing or a quick wit. The flip side is flightiness, a tendency to blow hot and cold, or to mask real feelings behind a jokey "don't get too serious" attitude.

HEALTH A fast metabolism and a tendency to run off nervous energy but bounce back easily from minor ailments. Prone to problems with the respiratory system, the shoulders, arms, or hands, including repetitive strain or other muscular injury.

FAMOUS GEMINI ASCENDANTS

Reba McEntire, Mick Jagger, Sandra Bullock,
Drew Barrymore, Gene Wilder, Kiri Te Kanawa

♋ CANCER ASCENDANT
OR THE MOON IN THE 1ST HOUSE

With a Cancer Ascendant, regardless of the Sun sign, the ruling planet of the horoscope is the Moon. This planet's sign and house will be a primary consideration in the process of interpretation.

PHYSICAL CHARACTERISTICS Amiable and mobile features, highly expressive, roundness in the face, "apple" cheeks—sometimes fleshy—full lips, and a wide smile, crinkly or luminous eyes, either large and round or deep-set, experts at the sideways glance.

MANNER AND SPEECH Can come across as evasive, ironic, courteous, or cautious. As with all the water signs, the approach to new people or situations is somewhat guarded or tentative as they check their findings on an emotional or slightly suspicious barometer. Outwardly, however, this is hard to detect. Individuals with this rising sign or 1st house Moon tend to converse in soft, even tones that express interest and concern, naturally steering the conversation away from themselves and deflecting intimacy until they are ready to drop their guard.

HEALTH A highly sensitive gut, susceptible to acid stomach and intolerance to particular foods. Prone to inherited conditions or problems in the chest/breast area. The women may also be susceptible to gynecological ailments, especially uterine.

FAMOUS CANCER ASCENDANTS

Angelina Jolie, Matt LeBlanc, Cameron Diaz,
John Travolta, Judy Garland, Kate Hudson

♌ LEO ASCENDANT
OR THE SUN IN THE 1ST HOUSE

With a Leo Ascendant, regardless of the Sun sign, the ruling planet of the horoscope is the Sun. This planet's sign and house will be a primary consideration in the process of interpretation.

PHYSICAL CHARACTERISTICS Well-built and sturdy body, often athletic. The classic leonine look can be even stronger than for those with Sun in Leo, notably the broad face, neat or wide-tipped nose, and thick or shaggy mane. Excellent posture is also a distinctive feature.

MANNER AND SPEECH Can come across as pompous, warmly welcoming, confident, or commanding. Often they fear ridicule, and they are the experts at assuming a regal manner and putting on a brave face. Individuals with this rising sign or 1st house Sun are also natural organizers or entertainers, and have a knack for being at the center of things. They love drama and are quite capable of creating one when life gets too tame, but they are big-hearted loyalists and will always rise to the occasion, whether it is a celebration or a crisis.

HEALTH Generally a "love of life" resilient constitution, although prone to back problems or disc injuries. A strong heart but susceptible to cardiac problems in later life unless mindful of a "healthy heart" regime of diet and exercise.

FAMOUS LEO ASCENDANTS

Luciano Pavarotti, Marilyn Monroe, Christopher Reeve, Beyoncé Knowles-Carter, Tina Turner, Taylor Swift

---

♍ VIRGO ASCENDANT
OR MERCURY IN THE 1ST HOUSE

With a Virgo Ascendant, regardless of the Sun sign, the ruling planet of the horoscope is Mercury. This planet's sign and house will be a primary consideration in the process of interpretation.

PHYSICAL CHARACTERISTICS Often a youthful vibe, square head or face, girlish or boyish features that tend to be on the small side but well proportioned, deep-set but lively or questioning eyes, sometimes a prominent forehead.

MANNER AND SPEECH Can come across as superior, critical, inquisitive, or particular. With this rising sign or a 1st house Mercury, everything is put through an analytical sieve until an exact understanding of a person, situation, or task has been reached. They generally take nothing as gospel without checking it out for themselves. They have painstaking patience, superb attention to detail, and a talent for precision in the honing of their skills and crafts, but often set the bar too high in their expectations of others. Meticulous care over personal appearance is also a common characteristic.

HEALTH Health-consciousness is usually pronounced, especially in later years. Prone to conditions related to anxiety, intestinal problems, and food allergies.

FAMOUS VIRGO ASCENDANTS

Gene Kelly, Tiger Woods, Walt Disney, Paul Simon, Nicole Scherzinger, J. R. R. Tolkien

---

♎ LIBRA ASCENDANT
OR VENUS IN THE 1ST HOUSE

With a Libra Ascendant, regardless of the Sun sign, the ruling planet of the horoscope is Venus. This planet's sign and house will be a primary consideration in the process of interpretation.

PHYSICAL CHARACTERISTICS Often an indication of beauty, symmetrical and softly modeled features, usually a straight nose, a full or well-shaped mouth, sometimes dimples in the chin or cheeks, pleasant and kindly expression, often look younger than their years.

MANNER AND SPEECH Can come across as passive, indifferent, easygoing, or charming. Mostly the nature is extremely amiable, polite, and softly spoken in individuals with this rising sign or a 1st house Venus. They are naturals at engaging with others and would rather walk on hot coals than deliberately give offence. For this reason they tend not to air their personal views too soon or too energetically. Similarly, they are the first to placate others and to troubleshoot from a viewpoint of fairness and justice.

HEALTH Physical well-being rests largely on a balanced diet and emotional equilibrium. Prone to kidney problems, diabetes, or vacillating energy, sometimes related to highly sensitive blood sugar levels.

FAMOUS LIBRA ASCENDANTS

Jennifer Aniston, Omar Sharif, Britney Spears,
Denzel Washington, Leonardo DiCaprio, Barry Gibb

♏ SCORPIO ASCENDANT
OR MARS OR PLUTO IN THE 1ST HOUSE

With a Scorpio Ascendant, regardless of the Sun sign, the ruling planet of the horoscope is Mars, with Pluto as the co-ruler. These planets' signs and houses will be a primary consideration in the process of interpretation.

PHYSICAL CHARACTERISTICS Overt or subtle sexiness, chiseled features, beautiful eyes, often with a hypnotic or penetrating "X-ray" quality, frequently a slightly raised bridge to the nose, a brooding expression, and often heavy brows in the men.

MANNER AND SPEECH Can come across as reserved, private, formidable, or fascinating. They have phenomenal reserves of determination and their approach to life and relationships in particular is intense, emotional, and profound. Individuals with this rising sign, and especially a 1st house Pluto, need to forge deep connections and tend to give short shrift to those deemed to be flippant or superficial. New faces and situations are put through remorseless screening, and they attach great importance to their first impressions. Usually these are uncannily correct.

HEALTH Mostly resilient with exceptional powers of recuperation from illness or from over-doing things. Prone to problems with the reproductive or excretory systems.

FAMOUS SCORPIO ASCENDANTS

Diana Ross, Michael Douglas, Sigmund Freud,
Clint Eastwood, Rafael Nadal, Nicole Kidman

SAGITTARIUS ASCENDANT
OR JUPITER IN THE 1ST HOUSE

With a Sagittarius Ascendant, regardless of the Sun sign, the ruling planet of the horoscope is Jupiter. This planet's sign and house will be a primary consideration in the process of interpretation.

PHYSICAL CHARACTERISTICS Tall or big frames, especially the men, large hands and feet, long-limbed, a sporty physique, a swinging stride, a tendency to clumsiness, a prominent and sometimes "horsy" nose, deep-set but quizzical eyes, and a distinctive laugh.

MANNER AND SPEECH Can come across as friendly, tactless, enthusiastic, or larger than life. Generally there are no hidden agendas and what you see is what you get. Individuals with this rising sign or 1st house Jupiter tend to speak as they find, bestow trust easily, and consequently rarely suspect others of sinister motives. They intuitively put people or situations to the "is this interesting?" test, and quickly disengage when bored. The general approach to life is restless, adventurous, freedom-orientated, and optimistic.

HEALTH Generally a fortunate and robust constitution, but need to pace themselves in lifestyle and control the tendency to excess. Prone to problems with the liver and injuries or conditions affecting the hips, thighs, buttocks, or sciatic nerve.

FAMOUS SAGITTARIUS ASCENDANTS

Hilary Swank, Prince William, Catherine Zeta-Jones,
Elton John, Goldie Hawn, Elvis Presley

♑ CAPRICORN ASCENDANT
OR SATURN IN THE 1ST HOUSE

With a Capricorn Ascendant, regardless of the Sun sign, the ruling planet of the horoscope is Saturn. This planet's sign and house will be a primary consideration in the process of interpretation.

PHYSICAL CHARACTERISTICS Generally of a large or solid build, with squareness or distinctive planes to the face. Often striking bone structure, including the cheekbones, and a firm jaw, and prone to aging gracefully.

MANNER AND SPEECH Can come across as guarded, unsympathetic, gloomy, or proper. In youth they seem older than their years, but they seem younger in their outlook as they grow older. For individuals with this rising sign or 1st house Saturn, life often gets off to a tough start, either in terms of experiencing too much responsibility too soon or by being held back through hardship, oppression, or a rigid family culture, especially through the father. Winning respect and forging self-esteem, ideally through success in their vocation, softens their seriousness or pessimism.

HEALTH Exceptionally hardy constitution and powers of endurance. Prone to difficult-to-treat skin conditions, such as eczema or psoriasis, or aging ailments of bones and joints, especially the knees, such as rheumatism, arthritis, and osteoporosis.

FAMOUS CAPRICORN ASCENDANTS

Queen Elizabeth II, Sean Connery, Marie Curie,
Larry King, Sophia Loren, Susan Sarandon

♒ AQUARIUS ASCENDANT
♒ OR SATURN OR URANUS IN THE 1ST HOUSE

With an Aquarius Ascendant, regardless of the Sun sign, the ruling planet of the horoscope is Saturn, with Uranus as the co-ruler. These planets' signs and houses will be a primary consideration in the process of interpretation.

PHYSICAL CHARACTERISTICS Saturn types tend toward stockiness or heaviness; Uranus types often tend toward the opposite owing to hyperactivity; piercing, wide-set eyes, often a startling blue in fair-skinned types, high forehead, long straight nose, wide mouth, and big smile.

MANNER AND SPEECH Can come across as inquisitive, indifferent, original, or unusual. Individuals with this rising sign, and especially a 1st house Uranus, often have experiences early on in life that set them apart. This, in turn, makes for strong personalities that are very much a law unto themselves. This rising sign also denotes an incisive intelligence but some emotional jet lag, often from a "head-over-heart" upbringing. The initial response to new people or situations is extremely analytical, sometimes giving the impression of distance or coolness.

HEALTH Mostly physically robust, although prone to problems with circulation or injuries to the lower leg or ankles. The mind-body connection is particularly important; susceptible to acute depression when "split off" from their authentic selves.

FAMOUS AQUARIUS ASCENDANTS

Barack Obama, Whoopi Goldberg, Sylvia Plath,
Jay Leno, Roseanne Barr, Jim Morrison

♓ PISCES ASCENDANT
OR JUPITER OR NEPTUNE IN THE 1ST HOUSE

With a Pisces Ascendant, regardless of the Sun sign, the ruling planet of the horoscope is Jupiter, with Neptune as the co-ruler. These planets' signs and houses will be a primary consideration in the process of interpretation.

PHYSICAL CHARACTERISTICS Usually tall or big-boned, face tends to roundness and softness, liquid eyes, generally wide-set, sometimes protruding, especially in the men, highly mobile or malleable features, a gentle aura.

MANNER AND SPEECH Can come across as charming, vague, vulnerable, or compassionate. The approach to life and relationships is extremely tentative or hopelessly idealistic. Individuals with this rising sign, and especially a 1st house Neptune, can be impressionable and suggestible. Often there are early experiences of loss or of being exposed to a harsh reality that leaves them at the mercy of others. They understand suffering and find themselves through marine, musical, artistic, or altruistic vocations, or lose themselves through escapism or the inability to heal the victim's wounds.

HEALTH A sensitive constitution that needs peace of mind, body, and spirit. When troubled, suffers from insomnia or stress-related illnesses, extremely susceptible to adverse reactions to drugs, alcohol, or anesthesia, prone to problems with or injuries to the feet.

FAMOUS PISCES ASCENDANTS

George Clooney, Whitney Houston, Pope Benedict XVI, Demi Moore, Phil McGraw—aka Dr. Phil, Gwyneth Paltrow

THE HOUSES

As has been mentioned already, your horoscope (birth chart) includes not only the zodiac wheel, which is related to the Earth's yearly rotation around the Sun, but also a wheel of 12 houses. Houses are always measured from the Ascendant—the sign rising over the eastern horizon at the time of birth—and act as a 24-hour clock, with each house representing about 2 hours (see page 152 for more about the horoscope chart). The positions of the planets therefore can be described as being not only in a sign, but also in a house.

The concerns of each house are in keeping with the symbolism of the sign and planet(s) to which they correspond, and are numbered anti-clockwise. So, as with the signs and planets, each house has its own dominion, whether this be other people, work matters, health, money, and so on.

As we walk through the houses, we venture further into the machinery of the horoscope. Again, and more forcibly, we realize that our chart is not just about "me" in terms of personality, aptitude, or psychological makeup, but also about our world and the people, experiences, and concerns that play their roles in shaping our lives. Astrology starts to get very exciting at this stage as we discover that the threads of all our relationships and all our life events are part of the horoscope's rich tapestry.

1ST HOUSE

CORRESPONDING SIGN: **ARIES**
CORRESPONDING PLANET: **MARS**

The 1st house corresponds purely to the individual in terms of the physical body, appearance, ego, and sense of self. Here we find the individual at their moment of arrival, prior to any life experience.

The themes of the 1st house reflect the Aries key phrase of "I am."

2ND HOUSE

CORRESPONDING SIGN: **TAURUS**
CORRESPONDING PLANET: **VENUS**

The 2nd is the house of sustenance, that is, all that is needed for an individual to survive and thrive at a physical level. Here we locate personal money matters, possessions, and material goods. All that can be appreciated through the five senses is here, including food and all agricultural produce.

The themes of the 2nd house reflect the Taurus key phrase of "I possess."

3RD HOUSE
CORRESPONDING SIGN: GEMINI
CORRESPONDING PLANET: MERCURY

The 3rd is primarily the house of communication and encompasses everything connected to the written and spoken word—talking, writing, e-mails, letters, the media, phones, computers, conversation, ideas, thoughts, understanding, and so on. In terms of people, the 3rd house rules our siblings and neighbors. It is also our neighborhood, and it rules short-distance travel and all modes of local transport, such as cars, bikes, and buses. Traditional astrology calls this the house of "the lower mind," as it rules early education and mental development.

The themes of the 3rd house reflect the Gemini key phrase of "I speak."

4TH HOUSE
CORRESPONDING SIGN: CANCER
CORRESPONDING PLANET: THE MOON

Here we locate our home and family, where we live now but also our roots, origins, and the environment of our early upbringing. All property concerns belong here. In terms of people, the 4th house rules one of the parents but, even though the Moon and Cancer are more associated with the mother, traditional astrology does in fact give the 4th to the father. In reality, this varies from chart to chart, so the 4th can be either parent. Whether it is mother or father becomes apparent in the study of each individual horoscope.

The themes of the 4th house reflect the Cancer key phrase of "I secure."

5TH HOUSE
CORRESPONDING SIGN: **LEO**
CORRESPONDING PLANET: **THE SUN**

The 5th is the "fun house"—parties, hobbies, relaxation, holidays, and anything else enjoyable. This encompasses the extremes of hedonism, gambling, and risk taking. It is also the house of creativity, artistic flair, and all that we give life to. In terms of people, children belong to the 5th, those whom we create, and so do lovers, those with whom we share pure pleasure rather than serious commitment or the tougher demands of our world.

The themes of the 5th house reflect the Leo key phrase of "I create."

6TH HOUSE
CORRESPONDING SIGN: **VIRGO**
CORRESPONDING PLANET: **MERCURY**

The 6th is the house of work, from menial day-to-day jobs and chores to the expertise of crafts and skills. Health is also here, and all those who work in the health industry. This extends to all areas of service to others, so, in terms of people, servants, skilled labor, or anyone in our employ belong here. Those who serve their country are included in this category, too, so the 6th is also the house of the armed forces. Lodgers are here, as are pets and all small animals.

The themes of the 6th house reflect the Virgo key phrase of "I serve."

7TH HOUSE

CORRESPONDING SIGN: **LIBRA**
CORRESPONDING PLANET: **VENUS**

Here we start to find meaning through the rule of opposites. The 1st is the individual, so the 7th is the house of partnership and "the significant other," your other half, marriage, and all major, one-to-one relationships at either a personal or business level belong here. Traditional astrology also says that open enemies or opponents—anyone publicly against you—are to be located in this house.

The themes of the 7th house reflect the Libra key phrase of "I relate."

8TH HOUSE

CORRESPONDING SIGN: **SCORPIO**
CORRESPONDING PLANETS: **MARS AND PLUTO**

The 2nd house signifies personal means, so the 8th is the dominion of other people's money and resources, especially the partner's. This is also the house of death and goods of the deceased. The 8th rules sex in terms of the cycle of conception, birth, and decay, and also symbolic death, rebirth, and transformation. It is also the house of surgery and surgeons. This is an important house psychologically, as it rules the unconscious and all that is hidden or taboo. The 2nd is the house of the sensual and visible; the 8th is the house of the invisible and the sixth sense.

The themes of the 8th house reflect the Scorpio key phrase of "I regenerate."

9TH HOUSE
CORRESPONDING SIGN: **SAGITTARIUS**
CORRESPONDING PLANET: **JUPITER**

The 3rd represents early learning, so the 9th is known as the house of "the higher mind." Higher education, philosophy, the search for meaning, religion, truth, justice, and the law belong here, as well as all those who work in these fields, such as teachers, gurus, and priests. The 3rd is our neighborhood, so the 9th is the rest of the world, all things foreign, and those from overseas, freedom of movement, long-distance travel, and means of transport, especially planes. Publishing and serious literature also belong to this house.

The themes of the 9th house reflect the Sagittarius key phrase of "I seek."

10TH HOUSE
CORRESPONDING SIGN: **CAPRICORN**
CORRESPONDING PLANET: **SATURN**

The 4th represents our home and origins, so in the 10th we locate our place out in the world, our ambitions and aspirations, our public life, profession, and status, where we are going as opposed to where we come from. In terms of people, the other parent is here, often the breadwinner as opposed to the homemaker, as are all those who have authority over us, from bosses to monarchs.

The themes of the 10th house reflect the Capricorn key phrase of "I master."

11TH HOUSE

CORRESPONDING SIGN: **AQUARIUS**
CORRESPONDING PLANETS: **SATURN AND URANUS**

The 5th is the house of individual creativity and intimate relationships, so in the 11th we locate the wider circle of people in our lives. Friends, colleagues, peers, and equals are all found here. Anything that is linked to the collective belongs to this house, from our social life, groups, and societies, to all kinds of organizations and political systems. Along with our ideals, social values, and political beliefs, traditional astrology also calls the 11th the house of "hopes and wishes."

The themes of the 11th house reflect the Aquarian key phrase of "I understand."

12TH HOUSE

CORRESPONDING SIGN: **PISCES**
CORRESPONDING PLANETS: **JUPITER AND NEPTUNE**

Arguably the most difficult house, the 12th is traditionally known as the house of blind spots, ambushes, self-undoing, and the "vale of tears." In terms of people, the 12th is the dominion of hidden enemies, and also those who are lost to us through estrangement or early death. It is the house of sacrifices and seclusion, so places of confinement, such as hospitals or prisons, are located here. The most positive expression of this house is retreat in the pursuit of inner contemplation and karmic lessons, and those who devote their lives to the spiritual good of others.

The themes of the 12th house reflect the Pisces key phrase of "I redeem."

IN A NUTSHELL: HOUSES AS OPPOSITES

In terms of astrological symmetry, the houses work in pairs of opposites:

1ST HOUSE the Self
7TH HOUSE Significant Other

2ND HOUSE Personal finances, the resources for life
8TH HOUSE Shared finances, death, and goods of the dead

3RD HOUSE Communication, local environment, and early education for survival
9TH HOUSE Higher education and wider horizons, for experience and understanding

4TH HOUSE Home, family, and private life
10TH HOUSE Purpose and public life

5TH HOUSE Personal pleasures and creativity, children
11TH HOUSE Group pleasures and concerns, friends

6TH HOUSE Physical health, service
12TH HOUSE Spiritual life, sacrifice

THE QUADRANTS

The houses are also grouped into quadrants:

+ The first house of each quadrant is an angular house—1, 4, 7, and 10—
  so called because these houses mark the beginning of the four angles,
  the main axis of the horoscope. They correspond to the cardinal signs.
  Planets in these houses are at their most visible, active, and potent.
+ The second house of each quadrant is a succedent house—2, 5, 8,
  and 11—so called simply because these houses "succeed" or follow on
  from the angular houses. They correspond to the fixed signs.
+ The third house of each quadrant is a cadent house—3, 6, 9, and 12—
  so called because cadent means "falling," so they fall away from the main
  action, and these houses correspond to the mutable signs. Planets in
  these houses are said to be at their least visible or powerful.

NATURAL HOUSE

Note that if a planet is in its "own" house, that is, where it belongs in
the natural astrological pattern, it is said to be strengthened by being in
its natural house. For example, a 1st house Mars, a 2nd house Venus,
a 3rd house Mercury, and so on would all be natural house planets.

THE ANGLES

When you draw a line from the beginning of the 1st house to the
beginning of the 7th, and then from the beginning of the 4th to the
beginning of the 10th, the axis marks the important angles of the chart.
The subsequent division of the quadrants creates the trisections of the
inner house cusps and the twelve houses. The wheel of the horoscope
also acts as a 24-hour clock.

THE ASCENDANT: 6AM OR SUNRISE

Arguably the most important part of the horoscope, the Ascendant—or rising sign—is the sign rising over the eastern horizon at the time of birth. It therefore marks the beginning of the 1st house and is the front door into any horoscope.

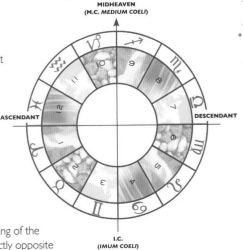

THE DESCENDANT: 6PM OR SUNSET

This angle marks the beginning of the 7th house and is always exactly opposite the Ascendant. This is where we locate any significant others in terms of partnership, whether personal or professional.

THE MIDHEAVEN: MIDDAY

The Midheaven is also known as the M.C., which stands for *medium coeli*, which is Latin for "middle of the sky." This angle marks the beginning of the 10th house. In some horoscopes you will find this angle drawn as an arrow, pointing up toward the heavens. The Midheaven points to where we are going, symbolizing our vocation, status, and aspirations in life.

THE I.C.: MIDNIGHT

I.C. stands for *imum coeli*, which is Latin for "bottom of the sky," the sky below us. This angle is always exactly opposite the M.C., and it marks the beginning of the 4th house. It symbolizes our origins, where we have come from.

HOUSE RULERSHIP

When you first look at a horoscope, one of the first things you will notice is that certain houses are devoid of planets. This does not mean that the houses in question are inactive in any way. An empty 5th house, for example, does not indicate childlessness, just as an empty 7th house does not mean an absence of relationships. Matters pertaining to any house are described in two ways:

+ by any planets posited in the house
+ primarily by the planet that rules the house.

CHART RULER

As already stated, the ruling planet of any horoscope is the planet that rules the sign on the Ascendant. So, if Virgo is rising, the native will be ruled by Mercury; if Libra is rising, they will be ruled by Venus, and so on. When considering the three signs that have a co-ruler (Scorpio, Aquarius, and Pisces), always take the traditional planet as the primary significator and the co-ruler as the secondary. For example, if Pisces is rising, the native will be ruled by Jupiter and secondly by Neptune, the co-ruler.

One of the first vital steps in interpretation is to locate and assess the "condition" of the chart ruler; that is, to determine how strong or weak the planet may be in terms of sign and house.

HOUSE RULERS

The same scrutiny applies to the ruling planet of each house. For example:

+ If we find Sagittarius on the 2nd house cusp, then the native's financial concerns will be described by the condition (sign, house, aspects) of Jupiter.
+ If we find Capricorn on the 2nd house cusp, then the native's financial concerns will be described by the condition of Saturn.
+ If we find Aries on the 7th house cusp (the Descendant), then the type of partner/the nature of relationships will be described by the condition of Mars.
+ If we find Gemini on the 7th house cusp, then the type of partner/the nature of relationships will be described by the condition of Mercury, and so on.

Understanding the principle of house rulership is therefore absolutely crucial to the art of chart interpretation. Once you adopt this system, you can locate absolutely anyone or anything in the horoscope. Essentially, this part of astrological craft enables you to ask not just "what is this planet telling me?" in terms of the native's own character and life situation, but also "who is this planet in the native's life?" As above, so below—the planet will describe the concerns of, or the people belonging to, the house in question.

IN A NUTSHELL: WHO IS WHERE

Each house indicates a relationship of the native (ruler of the 1st house) to others. Here is a reminder of where to find others in the horoscope.

2ND AND 8TH HOUSES
These houses are not used to locate others.
The 8th rules over the dead; the 2nd is the house of possessions, money, and disposable assets.

✦

3RD HOUSE
Brothers/sisters/neighbors:
Siblings and all taken-for-granted relationships in our immediate environment.

✦

4TH AND 10TH HOUSES
Parents:
Parents are indicated by the M.C./I.C. axis, the ancestral time line. Tradition gives the 4th to the father, the 10th to the mother, but this is a variable rule. Those who have authority over us are also shown by the 10th.

✦

5TH HOUSE
Children/lovers:
Those with whom we play, create, and simply enjoy being.

6TH HOUSE
Employees/servants/lodgers/doctors:
Those who are unequal to us, who do our bidding and attend us.

✦

7TH HOUSE
Significant others:
Close partners and all important one-to-one relationships—love, marriage, business—as well as open enemies, i.e. those who oppose the native.

✦

9TH HOUSE
Teachers/lawyers/priests and gurus:
All those whom we might seek out for help and guidance.

✦

11TH HOUSE
Friends/peers/colleagues and associates:
Our wider circle of friends and acquaintances—equals with whom we exchange views. All groups and those to whom we are related by a common interest or social brotherhood.

✦

12TH HOUSE
Secret enemies/jailors/spies:
Those who are against us or who confine us, or those who are lost to us.

CHAPTER 4
INTERPRETING HOROSCOPES

Each person's data—date, place, and time of birth—yields a unique horoscope or "nativity." Think of this as a photograph of the heavens that captures the position of the planets and angles at the precise moment of birth and as seen from the precise location on planet Earth. We start to appreciate the multifaceted depths of astrology only as we piece together all the information provided in this horoscope.

CHART CALCULATION

o- -o

If you simply type "calculating your horoscope," any search engine will direct you to astrology sites that offer this service and are quick and easy to use. Entering your date, place, and time of birth will produce the visual of your personal horoscope, showing you the degree and sign of your Ascendant and the exact position of all the planets on the wheel. The site I recommend is www.astrotheme.com/horoscope_chart_sign_ascendant.php.

If you do not know your time of birth, simply enter 12.00 midday. This will produce what is known as a Noon Chart. While this chart will not be wholly accurate in terms of the Ascendant and the position of the Moon—the swiftest-moving body—you will still be able to learn the sign and degree held by the other planets. Throughout this book you will find several examples of celebrities, whose birth times are not known, to illustrate how accurate this can be.

Looking at your horoscope online is sufficient for finding out which planet is in which sign for any date of birth, but for the serious student I strongly recommend drawing up the horoscope in your own hand. You need only a stack of blank wheels divided into twelve sections, which you can either make yourself or buy from any astrology shop. This will speed up your "connection" with each horoscope.

UNDERSTANDING THE VISUAL LAYOUT

Let us start with a quick, "back to school" mathematical reminder of the relationship between time and space:

+ A clock face contains 360 degrees that are divided into 12 hours. Each hour contains 60 minutes (of time), and each minute contains 60 seconds (of time).
+ The wheel of the horoscope contains 360 degrees and, as there are 12 signs of the zodiac, each sign contains 30 degrees. Each degree contains 60 minutes (of space), and each minute contains 60 seconds (of space).

SIZE OF THE HOUSES AND INTERCEPTED SIGNS

There is a variety of "house systems" from which to choose, which means slightly different ways of dividing up the 360 degrees of the horoscope, but the most widely used system is called Placidus. As with most of the house systems, Placidus does not operate on the "equal house" system, which gives exactly 30 degrees to each house. House sizes are variable, every single chart is unique, and the actual size of the houses is determined astronomically by the date, time, and place of birth of the individual.

The houses do not need to be drawn to scale. The circle is simply divided into 12 sections and the number/sign on each house cusp tells you the starting point of each house. The left-hand side and the right-hand side of

all horoscopes are always exactly symmetrical, so the 1st house is exactly the same size as the 7th, the 2nd the same as the 8th, and so on. The cusp—the point at which the house begins—of the 1st house always appears at the midpoint on the left side of the chart.

Occasionally, you will find that some of the individual houses are so big that they take up considerably more than a 30-degree space. This can result in "intercepted signs," whereby one house will include a whole sign that is then flanked by the late degrees of the previous sign and the early degrees of the next.

IS YOUR CHART CORRECT?

There is no denying that computer packages save us hours of work and mathematical headaches. Bear in mind, though, that software is only ever as good as the person using it. It is easy to enter incorrect data, especially in relation to time zones. In order to avoid using a chart that has been generated from incorrect data, here is a quick "look-see" way to check that you have ended up with the right chart.

The horoscope represents a 24-hour clock and the Sun acts as a marker. The Sun is nearly always positioned in or next to the house that relates to the time of birth. This can vary slightly in some time zones, but even so the Sun will be no further than one house either way.

For example, if you have a birth time of 9.00am, the Sun will be in the 11th house (the section of the chart that relates to 08.00–10.00am); if you have a birth time of 9.00pm, the Sun will be in the 5th house (the section of the chart that relates to 8.00–10.00pm).

You may find that this varies slightly when the time falls close to a house cusp. For example, if you have a birth time of 10.00am, then the Sun will be in either the 10th or 11th house; if it is further away—say in the 9th or the 12th—you will know instantly that the chart is incorrect.

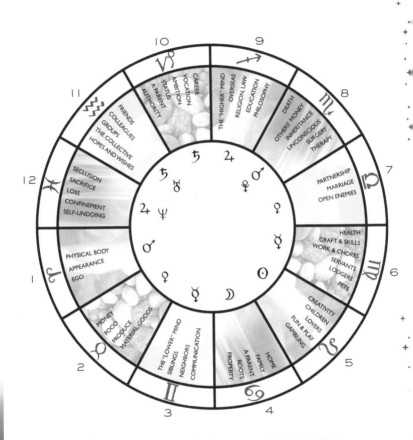

This image provides a reminder of the houses—their associated signs (on the outside), planets (in the middle of the wheel), and concerns.

CHART INTERPRETATION

o--o

In order to interpret a chart fully, in addition to looking at signs, planets, and houses, an astrologer also needs to look at the aspects—the position of planets in relation to one another. As this book provides only an introduction, the aspects aren't covered here, but you can still work with the symbolism of the signs, the nature of the planets, the meaning of the houses, and the importance of house rulership to equip yourself with the tools of the craft needed to make the leap into the world of chart interpretation. (For suggested reading on going further with astrology, see page 160.)

Every serious student of astrology, without exception, can reach the point of being technically knowledgeable but will still struggle with the challenge of translating the symbolism so that it "speaks" in an accurate and meaningful way. In many ways we find ourselves learning a foreign language, and just because we have some vocabulary and grammar under our belts does not mean that we can automatically make the leap to fluency.

Absolutely the first principle to remember is that there is a substantial limit on what we can "know" in advance. This is because astrological symbolism works at two levels—the universal and the particular. For example:

+ At a **universal** level, we know that Mars symbolizes our drive, libido, anger, and so on. Most astrological literature and websites operate at this level, which is why, when you read a supposed definition of a planet in a sign or any astrological feature, it will more often than not fall short of the "truth."

- At a **particular** level, Mars will have a far more specific role to play in any given horoscope depending on his "condition"—his position by sign, house, and aspects in relation to the other planets. He will signify other people or issues in the native's life depending on the houses that he rules.

Ultimately, and most importantly, how Mars plays out for any individual can be interpreted only when seen in context. The astrologer's task is to listen to the client's "story" and to locate that story in the symbolism of the chart.

LOCATING SIGNIFICANCE

Locating significance is a phrase coined by Geoffrey Cornelius and Maggie Hyde, founders of The Company of Astrologers. This is an approach that teaches us how to sidestep the laborious and ultimately pointless exercise of making reams and reams of notes, which may look impressive on paper, but which in reality are usually of little use, especially when face to face with a client. Locating significance simply means finding the meaning by zooming in on what is important in every individual horoscope. It is at this stage that we truly understand the value of knowing our astrological "grammar and vocabulary" and come to appreciate that the art of chart interpretation rests on a bedrock of sound technical knowledge.

YOUR ASTROLOGICAL CHECKLIST

By following these guidelines, you can start to unlock the content and possible meaning of any given horoscope.

THE HOROSCOPE VISUAL Most astrologers these days print their horoscopes straight from their computers, drawn up by their software. Call me old-fashioned, but, although I use a computer package to do my mathematics for me, I always draw up my charts in my own hand. I strongly advise that you adopt this habit, especially in the early days of study. It is a deeply satisfying ritual at a creative or artistic level, and, more importantly, the experience of seeing the chart take shape under your own pen will automatically guide you to what is important. When you have finished drawing up your chart, you will feel an immediate "relationship" with it, something that is harder to achieve when looking at a computer-generated printed chart.

START WITH THE OBVIOUS—THE ANGLES Is there anything yelling for attention, for example, a planet on an angle (the Ascendant/Descendant or the M.C./I.C.)? Jennifer Lopez (b. July 24, 1969) is a textbook Leo—and a double one. The Sun at 1 degree of Leo sits exactly on her Ascendant, also at 1 degree of Leo: born to perform to an adoring public.

LOCATE THE CHART RULER Assess its condition by sign and house.

MISSING ELEMENTS Note if there is a missing element among the personal planets, Sun to Saturn. This does not mean that the native lacks the qualities associated with the element. It would obviously be nonsense to say, for example, that someone with no water has no feelings. We all have feelings. Rather, a missing element often symbolizes something that was absent, discouraged, or ignored in the person's upbringing, and therefore something that we have to figure out for ourselves. See box opposite for some examples as discovered through my own client work.

MISSING ELEMENTS GUIDE

No fire: a lack of value placed on spontaneity, risk taking, or the child's individuality, experiences that sabotaged confidence

No earth: a lack of money, physical or emotional security, or instruction regarding survival skills

No air: a lack of encouragement with learning, no interest or value placed on the child's expression of personal views or ideas

No water: a lack of regard for the child's feelings, a family culture of devaluing or suppressing emotions

It is by no means a hard-and-fast rule, but when you discover an element to be missing, check the Descendant. It is astonishing how often that element is on this important angle, as it very often symbolizes what is missing within and therefore what is sought from "the other."

MUTUAL RECEPTIONS This indicates a positive relationship between two planets that occupy each other's signs, even if they are not in aspect. For example, Venus in Sagittarius (Jupiter's sign) and Jupiter in Libra (Venus' sign) would be considered a cooperative partnership. An especially helpful exchange is indicated when the mutual reception involves two planets in detriment/fall but in each other's sign of dignity—for instance, Moon in Capricorn (detriment, but Saturn's sign of dignity) and Saturn in Cancer (fall, but the Moon's sign of dignity). Mutual receptions often signal the option of a move to be made, a "swapping over" from one path to another.

BIBLIOGRAPHY AND FURTHER READING

+ *Astrology for Beginners*, Maggie Hyde and Geoffrey Cornelius (Icon Books Ltd, Penguin, Cambridge, 1995)

+ Astrotheme.com—website of data for celebrity horoscopes

+ *Chiron and the Healing Journey: An Astrological and Psychological Perspective*, Melanie Reinhart (Starwalker Press, London, 2010)

+ *Christian Astrology*, William Lilly (Regulus Publishing Co. Ltd., 1985)

+ *Eclipses: The Power Points of Astrology*, Derek Appleby and Maurice McCann (The Aquarian Press, Wellingborough, Northamptonshire, 1986)

+ *Horary Astrology Rediscovered*, Olivia Barclay (Whitford Press, Schiffer Publishing Ltd., Atglen, Pennsylvania, 1990)

+ *Jung and Astrology*, Maggie Hyde (The Aquarian Press, London, 1992)

+ *The Karmic Journey: The Birthchart, Karma and Reincarnation*, Judy Hall (Arkana, Penguin, London, 1990)

+ *The Moment of Astrology*, Geoffrey Cornelius (Arkana, Penguin, London, 1994)

+ *The Principles of Astrology*, Charles E. O. Carter (The Theosophical Publishing House, Wheaton, Illinois, 1963)

+ *Profiles of Women*, Lois M. Rodden (The American Federation of Astrologers, Inc., Tempe, Arizona, 1979)

+ *Relating*, Liz Greene (The Aquarian Press, Wellingborough, Northamptonshire, 1986)

+ *Saturn: A New Look at an Old Devil*, Liz Greene (Samuel Weiser, Inc., York Beach, Maine, 1976)

+ *Secrets from a Stargazer's Notebook*, Debbi Kempton Smith (Bantam Books, New York, 1982)